★

It all starts with one wish.

The HISTORY of WISHES

Wish Making Rituals & Symbols from Around the World

TATIANA COLHOUN

THE HISTORY OF WISHES
18° 31' 05"N | 64° 22' 56"W

Visit us online at:
tatianacolhoun.com

Close your eyes
and make a wish.

Within all of us is a whispering voice
filling our minds with curiosity
longing to understand the fabric of life
and the starry heavens above.

INSPIRATION

I am an eternal optimist and lover of dreams. As far back as I can remember I have filled my life with wishes. Wishes for hope. Wishes for love and inner bliss. Wishes for peace on earth. Wishes that everyone would take a leap of faith and ignite that spark within their souls to pursue their passions and make all their dreams come true.

My inspiration lies in the skies above, fuelling my curiosity with all the beauty that we can see and all that we cannot. Every night I make a point of looking up at the sky. When I see all the stars, I envision a vast well of infinite pure souls and I remind myself of how blessed we all really are to be part of such an absolutely magnificent universe. Even though the stars are light years away, we are able to see them with our very own eyes. I believe that not only can they see us as well, but they too can hear and feel our wishes. Every night I close my eyes and make my wish for the universe to hear.

I believe we are all on a journey - we all have a purpose. And on this journey we continually meet people who also have wishes, hopes and dreams. Some inspire our lives and some need our inspiration. Fulfilling our dreams give feelings of accomplishment, success, self-worth, meaning, purpose, and so much more. Every person in this world counts. Every wish counts. Let's make this world a better place by filling it with dreams that are beyond imaginable. Imagine if we all wished more. Imagine if we all pursued our dreams. Imagine the world that we would live in.

And it all starts with one wish.

We would not silently pray
if there was nothing to pray for.
We would not secretly wish
if there was nothing to wish for.

CONTENTS

Anything is possible
if you put your mind to it.

HISTORY OF WISHES

There is something alchemistic and alluring about making a wish. The whole concept of wish making and its speculative nature of combining physics and science, philosophy and nature into one, whereby taking common elements and turning them into something beyond conceivable. Making a wish is at the root of all beings and ingrained in our souls. It's like we instinctively know what to do before we make one. In an instant we are able to clear our minds and begin the process of believing that anything is possible. We confidently make the wish and we put it out for the universe to hear.

A wish can be made in just a few seconds or over a span of several minutes. It is the origin of a spark for any idea. Wishes come in many sizes. They don't have to be elaborate or grand. But when we do make a wish, we reveal our innermost desires and ultimate dreams, quite often revealing what we really want to experience or achieve in our lifetime and more often than not, not what we are actually doing with our lives.

Wishing is a major 'hidden' or unseen component of our everyday existence and genetic makeup linked to the universe in such an intricate and highly detailed manner. Wishing has its own inertia using the powers and influence of energy, the Law of Attraction, and the hidden elements within life itself. Wishing energy is infinite in abundance, ever constant, and never expires. Wishing has always been, and will always be, rooted in the fundamental structure of our cosmos and still is today – we've just become preoccupied and distracted by other false trappings and we've simply forgotten how to harness the powers on the whole.

To most, wishing defies all rational explanation, yet wish making rituals predate recorded history and have held great significance to those before us. For thousands of years wishing rituals have occurred across our globe marked by endless sacred places, the bestowing of offerings, and symbolic wish representations across all ancient societies, cultures, religions, and more. Through the process of revisiting these ancient wishing rituals and understanding their importance, combined with our own inherent natural powers from within our own souls, I believe we can reopen the doors to once again tap in to the intangible powers of wishing. Recall the vision of Hermes, and *"Remember that the law of mystery veils the great truth"*.

There is so much to discover, and rediscover, in this beautiful universe of ours. My wish is for you to start tuning in, strengthening your non-physical and physical connections, exploring your creative side, and simply commit to keeping your passions in alignment with your actions. We all have an inner voice that fuels our everyday lives through passion, creativity and freedom of expression and I believe we are all born with the power to make our wishes come true. If you can dream it, it can be done.

My father always told me, *"Anything is possible if you put your mind to it"*. It is those few simple words that have powered my drive to want to do more, contribute more, dream up and make the impossible possible, ultimately contributing my share of making the world a better place.

WISHING RITUALS

Wish making rituals appear to have been in existence since the creation of humanity – it is part of our souls, our makeup, and our creative essence. Today there is a stark contrast between how our ancient ancestors perceived wish making and how it is perceived today. In ancient times, wish making was a sacred ritual. Somewhere along the way we somehow lost the strength in our ethereal connections. We need to rekindle the art of wish making. Everything in the universe is interconnected - past, present, future, and we need to begin reconnecting the dots. We have the potential. We have the power. All we have to do is believe.

The power of the human spirit
There is a strong correlation for when we believe something has significance and the creation of rituals – it's human nature. Rituals represent the extra preparation we are willing to take or devote to a given activity. Sometimes we are not able to define the origin of a ritual, as the ritual itself may be part and parcel of our inherent characteristics as humans. Wishing rituals however, all have one thing in common – the power of the human spirit and the ability to visualize and put out to this vast universe of ours our wishes, hopes and dreams from our innermost souls.

The universe is so immense and we have only just begun to unravel a minute fraction of its mysteries. The more we begin to truly tune in, connect and understand, the more the universe will gently begin to release additional information and allow us to discover all that we have been longing for.

Symbols & superstitions or hidden science?

Wishing rituals come in all shapes, forms and sizes. What do they all mean? Are they simply symbols and superstitions, or actual hidden science? Why do we think "it's just a wish" but we keep on wishing? Do we minimize the power of our thoughts, visions, wishes and dreams? And if we continue to minimize them, why do we keep wishing? Why not forget it all?

I strongly believe that wishing is, in fact, a hidden science we have yet to uncover. Many great scientific hypotheses have been realized through imagination and the power of intuition. Wish making also uses the same powers of imagination and intuition, and we need to learn how to harness them just like we would with any other technique we are trying to learn.

Children easily grasp the concept and know the power of a wish, so why as we age do we lose trust and allow these natural powers to fade? Why as adults do we lose faith in the whole concept? As children I find we are more open to receiving, but as we grow older and cross life's winding paths and challenges, we tend to become less 'open' and close our ever expansive and expressive minds. We dampen our creative thoughts and tend to view life differently. But why? What exactly changes as we grow older? Why do we lose hope? Are we taught to suppress our inner truths and feelings or are we simply disheartened by the lack of wishful life experiences?

Imagine if we all kept our minds consistently open as we once did as children? Imagine if we were all completely open to trying and learning with no fears or worries? If you are looking to make a change in your life, it is important to make a sincere effort and rekindle those childhood virtues. Never underestimate the value of the assets of a young mind that predictably remains more open and carefree. You may never know where to go until you take that offbeat path and expand your horizons. So be open to trying something new, explore the unknown, and create new tracks.

Is the term 'wishing' stigmatized?

I find it fascinating that we spend much our lives praying, dreaming, and having remarkable visions of how we can all improve our lives both personally and as a whole – all concepts being synonymous with wishing. They are in fact the same thing, but we tend to use different terms and avoid using the stigmatized term 'wishing'. Have you ever noticed as soon as you mention the word 'wishing' to someone, the word itself has evolved to lack reality and credibility? It is quite possible for this reason that most hesitate to share their wishes and innermost desires - for fear of being judged.

Ironically, the creation and origin of wishful thoughts put into action is what makes our personal lives and societies move forward. Every great past revolution has been sparked by wishes, visions, and desires to accelerate and explore better, faster, stronger technologies. Wishing acts as a catalyst and is the driver that pushes us forward. Every single thing you see in our world today would not be here had it not been for someone with a strong desire and motivation. And all these inventions and creations worldwide throughout the history of humankind began with just one wish.

But my dear,
you are the alchemist.

WHEN YOU WISH

Often when something so simple is before us we don't take notice. And it is the simplest of things that frequently may contain the most remarkable of rewards. The power of wishing is one of those things. Wishes can be made anytime, anywhere, and with anything. Wishes are not only mobile, but adaptable as well. When you wish or long for something, your mind enters into a different state in its own realm.

Wishing also demands concentration. When you wish, you temporarily 'remove' yourself from the reality of your current life. You activate the part of your mind that can create and envision anything you want it to – and you are also able to envision it through to completion. When you wish, you let your mind wander to places it sometimes has never been to or even seen before. And at the same time, wishing fills your heart and soul with that warm, fuzzy feeling of delight and true inner bliss. You can picture the success of completing your wish, and the way it makes you feel is like no other. It's almost indescribable. It's like a natural high. Euphoric.

Wish making would have no significance or purpose if we lacked the sustenance to enjoy it and realize the benefits. How lucky are we to have been blessed with the will to achieve such incredible and remarkable things? Life, as we know it, has given us the capacity to wish and the capacity to create. No other living being here on earth can challenge the potential we have as human beings. When we wish we create inner drive and purpose, and we exercise hope. No matter how big or small our wishes may be, we are able to bring them to life for the benefit of not only ourselves, but to also share with others.

The fifth element

Wishing is rooted in the fundamental structure of our universe and is literally in our genes. What I find remarkable is the fluid nature of wishes and the ability to tap into the 'pure air' (or the fifth element – aether) to bring back certain pieces of serendipitous information to assist us on our journeys. Wishes have an illusive appearance and once we make our wishes and release them, it often feels like they have disappeared into thin air. We cannot physically see where they will go or know what will eventually happen with them, but what we often fail to see is that the universe does hear our wishes and is holding on to them for us all. The universe truly wants us to fulfill our innermost dreams. The universe wants us to succeed. So know that as long as you want to pursue your wishes, the universe will hold them close and assist you along the way.

Wishing also has the ability to heighten our awareness and connect us to the metaphysical as it relates to the transcendent, or to the certain reality beyond what may be perceptible to our human senses. Quite often we tend to perceive the act of wishing or praying as a connection to the 'creator', the universe, or the spiritual essence. The additional creation of related rituals heightens or strengthens our connectivity and brings us closer to where our souls come from or originate.

We create wishing rituals to assist us in fine-tuning our thoughts and brain waves to be in complete alignment with that of the frequencies and natural pulse of our universe. Wishing rituals act as synchronous reminders of the eternal essence of our souls within the universe. Experiencing heightened connections may also bring us potential answers and the guidance we need to fulfill our goals. When we come across or find an object related to a wishing ritual we instantly tune into it and understand the meaning behind its presence. These subtle reminders provided by the universe build faith, hope, trust and confidence relating directly to our wish journey revealing to us that we are on the right path.

When it matters most

We often wish when it matters most. It seems like when all else fails around us, a simple wish can help in putting it all back together again. There is great truth in this perception. Wishing restores faith and provides hope and trust that we are part of a bigger picture and that we are being cared for. Being able to wish beyond the impossible or unimaginable gives life both purpose and meaning. It creates hope for a better tomorrow. It is also interesting to note that some of our innermost wishes seem to be so simple, but remarkably common, and often representative of what money cannot buy – love, health, peace, and happiness or inner bliss.

Will we be able to uncover the hidden science behind wishing in our lifetime? We may never know the answer to this question, but one thing we do know is that the more we practice something, the better we get at it. Therefore, the more we wish and send our innermost thoughts and desires out into the vast universe, the more in tune we will be with our world.

Following are some of my favourite wish making rituals from around the world. Use these wish making ritual symbols and sacred places as daily reminders to follow your heart, follow your passions, and put your wishes out to the universe to hear. It's time to live your life with no regret, heal your soul, and live a life where you truly feel fulfilled from the inside out.

I wish for
more wishes.

THE DANDELION WISH

As a child I remember picking the dandelions that were seeded in full bloom, closing my eyes, making a wish and blowing all the seeds in the wind. I would stand in silence praying that my wish would come true and watch each and every seed magically fly on their own special paths.

I remember being fascinated by the power of this beautiful plant and its ability to grant wishes. All it takes is one wish and then nature simply takes care of the rest by separating each seed and multiplying your wish over and over again sending it far and wide. In essence, Mother Nature hears your wish and puts it out to the universe for you. And each of the seeds will land in the paths of others who may 'help' your wish come true along the way. What an incredible concept.

The origin of the Dandelion Wish is still a mystery. It's a tradition that can be found worldwide in numerous cultures. It is a common childhood memory favourite for many. The common folklore proposes that if you close your eyes, make a wish, then blow the seeds in the air, your wish will come true.

A magical plant
The dandelion has long been thought of as a magical plant. The plant has many medicinal properties to assist in healing medical ailments such as infections and disease, with claims of divination. Its natural healing capabilities have created an additional alchemistic element of influencing good luck, hope, romance, and the ability to make wishes come true.

Resilience

Dandelions are resilient plants. They grow very successfully when the flowers turn to seed and the numerous seeds are able to travel extremely long distances using Mother Nature's wind to spread them far and wide. Dandelions are much like the human spirit. Our souls are extremely resilient even if we don't feel so at all times. Our subconscious thoughts, innermost hopes and even fears are able to travel long distances as well, as long as we put them out there for the universe to hear.

One thought, one hope, one wish, one dream - all have the ability to multiply when received by the collective soul. Putting these parts of our soul out there is what allows us to grow as individuals, much like the seeds of a dandelion. The more faith we have in our wishes coming true and the more we nurture them, the stronger we become and the less fear we have in creating another wish.

Conceptualize spreading seeds with spreading wishes. When planting seeds we plant numerous seeds, not just one, as not all seeds take. The same can be said of wishes. Not all wishes may be possible at any given time, but if we don't plant the seeds and tend to them, we will never know which ones will take.

Every seed that you plant needs to be nurtured. You must create your own personal habitual pattern to take care of each seed and satisfy all the needs. All things must be taken into consideration right from inception such as location, environment, type of soil, how much light and water is required and more. There are so many variables involved for each and every type of seed that you need to research and acquire knowledge in order to be successful at reaping the rewards. Being prepared right at the very foundation when creating the root is extremely important. Creating this type of discipline is what allows the seed to grow and become fruitful. The same can be said for making wishes. In order for your wishes to come true you must develop and create positive habits and discipline at the root level.

Once you plant a seed, you are continuously tending to it and waiting in anticipation to the share the 'plant to be' with others to enjoy. Think of the concept of planting flowers. Once they are in full bloom, they are beautiful to the eye with all the possible colours and textures, and give off such wonderful scents for all living things to enjoy. Everyone is able to reap the benefits including bees, insects and more. We are essentially able to touch all the senses of so much more than we originally expected. Planting seeds, much like making wishes, is good for the soul and seeing the outcome of your hard work has incredible positive psychological payback. The benefits are numerous.

Share your wishes
Sharing our wishes can be the best part. When we share our wishes with others it often creates a spark in them to fulfill their own wishes as well. The positive energy that can be created is unlimited. It demonstrates the power of belief - the power for a wish to come true. It inspires those along the way. The concept of wishing is quite remarkable in itself. And all it takes is one wish to start the process.

So the next time you seed a field of dandelions and you are with a friend, pick a dandelion that is in full bloom together. Then unitedly close your eyes, make a wish, blow the seeds into the air and allow the magic to unfold.

More hope.
More love.
More peace.
More dreams.

WISHBONES

The furcula - two small clavicles fused at the centre point, flawlessly symmetrical, a necessary solid base for the wing muscles enabling flight, found in birds and some prehistoric creatures and dinosaurs. In Latin furcula means "little fork", but to most it is commonly referred to as the wishbone.

Upon seeing a furcula, one cannot help but automatically think of wishing. Our first instinct is to find someone to make a wish with and pull it apart. In this wish making ritual, making a wish cannot be made alone. The wishbone requires two people to simultaneously make a wish in unison without letting each other know what your wishes are. Once you both make your wish, you must pull on each end of the wishbone until it breaks. The person whose wish will be granted is the person who ends up with the longer portion of the wishbone.

On rare occasions the break may be equal. In this rare instance, both your wishes will be granted. Incredible enough and as impossible as it may seem, I have broken more than one wishbone exactly in half with my wishing partner, so it is definitely possible to do so!

For those interested in the science behind a dried wishbone, the wishbone actually breaks due to the mechanical stress put on it when the collagen in the bone dries out and the pulling force is used. If you choose the thicker side of the wishbone and let your wishing partner do all the work, the stress induced on the wishbone on your wishing partner's side will ensure the odds are in your favour and the break will occur on their side.

The furcula & wishes

So when and where exactly did wishing on a furcula originate? The most common theory dates back to the Etruscans (768BC to 264BC) of ancient Italy. On an interesting note, the Etruscan civilization had its own unique language and writing structure that to this day remains only partially understood. With that being said, it has been postulated that the Etruscans were a notable and wealthy civilization that believed in divine powers and consultation with the gods. The Etruscan religion is also said to have been imparted to them by the seers.

The Etruscans performed alectryomancy, an ancient practice whereby using birds, namely roosters or chickens, to provide divine information through the use of grains and alphabetic letters. Scribes would record the pecking of seeds to be later interpreted by priests revealing divine messages and prophetic signs. The sacred bird would later be offered up for sacrifice, and the furcula would be preserved for viewing. The furcula was said to hold divine powers and people would come to stroke the bone and make a wish.

When the last Etruscan cities were amalgamated by Rome circa 100BC, the Romans expanded the tradition into the way we know it today. The furcula became the iconic wishbone symbolizing luck and good fortune.

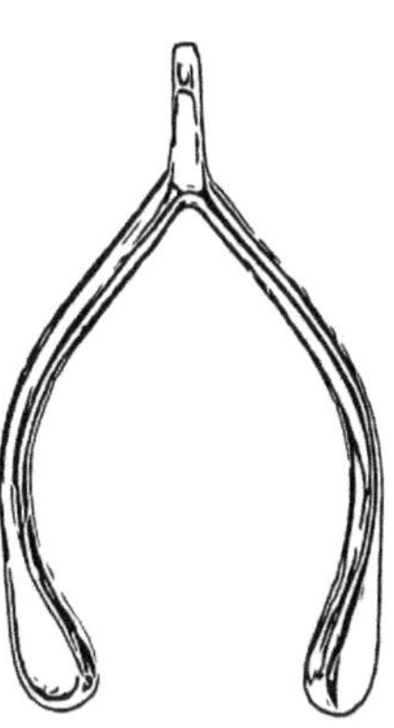

Follow your
own star.

WISHING ON STARS

Star light, star bright,
First star I see tonight,
I wish I may, I wish I might,
Have the wish I wish tonight.

Believed to be written in the late 19th century with American origins, *"Star Light, Star Bright"* became a popular nursery rhyme. This rhyme simply depicts the concept of people wishing on stars.

For centuries, people often look up at the night's sky, wondering what lies beyond our realm. There is something magical and whimsical about all those seemingly twinkling lights thousands of miles away. We are all blessed to be able to look up at the sky at night and experience what appears to be an incredible sea of diamonds.

Quite often in the evening, I will look up at the sky and wish upon the first star that I see and say this rhyme before making my wish. Remember, the stars are always there for you to wish upon – it's just the presence of the sun that dims their visibility during the day.

I am forever wishing on stars.

Star facts

When you look up at the night's sky have you ever wondered just exactly how many stars are there in our universe? Scientists say that there are more stars in the universe than all the grains of sand on our earth. Imagine that. I find it fascinating. Why are there so many? How were they formed? How can they shine so bright that we are able to see them over such great distances?

Stars have both a mystical quality and magical allure - so much so that for centuries it is believed that the stars kindly grant wishes to those who believe.

Following are some thought-provoking star observations:
- Stars signify the most basic building blocks of our galaxies.
- Located an average of 150 million kilometers away, the Sun is our closest star.
- Many stars orbit a mutual barycentre with other stars and come in pairs or multiples. Stars in pairs are called Binary Stars.
- At 4.37 light years from the Sun, Alpha Centauri is the closest star after the Sun and actually consists of 3 stars.
- The smallest and most abundant of stars are know as Red Dwarfs with lifespans of tens of billion of years.
- At approximately 7500 light years away, Eta Carinae is one of the largest, massive evolved stars classified as a Luminous Blue Variable Star. This colossal star may have up to 150 times the mass of the Sun with much debate over its evolution and potential lifespan.
- We are all made of stars and stardust. Echoing themes of fairy tales and poetry, this concept resonates with scientific theories behind a Supernova where the death of a star creates new life. Stardust from a Supernova scatters various elements across our universe ultimately creating new stars, new planets, and new life. All created from the heart of a star.

Astronomy, astrophysics & cosmology

Astronomy is known as the "Law of the Stars" or the "Culture of the Stars". One of the oldest natural sciences, astronomy is the study of celestial objects and galactic marvels outside the earth's atmosphere. Over time, astronomy expanded into various branches such as observational and theoretical. In general, astronomy traditionally refers to the qualitative aspect in the study of the celestial objects including their positions, motions, luminosities, and more.

Astrophysics, a branch of astronomy, refers to the physical nature of the stars and celestial objects as it relates to determining their nature, birth, life and death, rather than positions or motions. Astrophysics builds the physical theories of lesser to moderate sized configurations in the universe.

Cosmology, another branch of astrology, refers to the study of the universe as a whole, encompassing both its origin and evolution. Cosmology covers everything from dark matter and energy, to string theory and all the mysteries within.

Today modern astronomy also covers the physical aspects and overlaps both astrophysics and cosmology, and all of these terms now appear to be synonymous with one another or slightly blurred. The fascination with the stars, planets and galaxies has always been a source of curiosity and wonderment never losing its tenacity and spark. So many milestones have already been achieved in the study of astronomical objects and what lies beyond our earth's atmosphere.

According to astronomers, every star in our Milky Way may potentially have its own planet. Moreover, if that planet is in the right distance from a particular star, it may contain water – the key component to life. As we continue to move forward with our rapidly evolving technological and scientific evolution and understanding our place in the universe, we will mirror it with an innate desire to actually find life on other planets. I believe it is within our reach.

The origin of creation – building blocks, stars & stardust

According to science, stars signify the most basic building blocks of our galaxies. Similar to the Wishing Hour, the Number 1 and cells, stars are also known as the most basic building blocks. Remarkably, some of our most notable wishing rituals appear to be in alignment with the stars and have a common reoccurring theme as it relates to the notion of creation.

It is known that when you break down any organism into its most fundamental parts, the composition is consistent - carbon atoms connected to hydrogen, nitrogen, oxygen, phosphorus and sulphur. We also know that starlight is vital in the formation of chemicals that are precursors to the chemicals required to conceive life. This cosmic recipe often leads to the ever so popular question, *"Are we made of stars and stardust?"* We are indeed.

Recently, astronomers have itemized the abundance of these elements in a vast sample of hundreds of thousands of stars through spectroscopy. In fact, research teams even found unique chemical fingerprints within the stardust of young stars. The conclusion? It was concluded that stars and humans share common elements - just in different proportions to one another. The element proportions also differ between the stars themselves. In addition, the study helps with mapping the elements depending on the region within the galaxy.

So if we look at the elements for creation on the whole in our portion of the solar system, the concept indicates that if life was created on earth, then life was more than likely created on other planets. Maybe the reason why humans have always been so fascinated with the stars is that, in fact, we are all made of stardust and we cannot help but be captivated with our true source of origin and the unexplainable connection we feel from deep within.

Do the stars have souls?

So let's flip the question around and look at it from the other perspective. If humans are made of stars and stardust, do the stars have their own souls? Are all things including the stars and planets bestowed with souls that are living and thinking, guided by intelligence?

> *"Have the stars souls? Is the sun the tabernacle of a great spirit? Are the planets the bodies of divine intelligence? Ask the sun worshippers and the priests; ask the philosophers and the pundits and the modern men of learning. The ancients answer with one Voice, yes, and some of the moderns are not loath to echo this reply."*
>
> Do The Stars Have Souls
> Chicago Tribune, August 19, 1906

If the building blocks of life are found in stardust and the birth of new stars, whereby creating human life and our souls contained within our physical bodies, does that mean that souls are also integral to the creation process? Are souls floating free in the stardust? Do souls become contained in a 'physical body' (human, animals, nature or other things, such as a star or a planet) at the time of inception? I believe it is quite possible. Maybe souls are part of a bigger consciousness, like waves to the ocean. There are individual waves yet they would not be possible unless they were part of the ocean. We need to learn how to see from the 'inside' out.

My heart has always told me that our souls are part of a bigger connection – something astronomically bigger. It has been said that every human is a little world – a mikros cosmos. Proclus Lycaeus, a Greek Neo-Platonist philosopher, stated the concept eloquently:

> *"For, just like the Whole, he possesses both mind and reason, both a divine and a mortal body. He is also divided up according to the universe. It is for this reason, you know, that some are accustomed to say that his consciousness corresponds with the nature of the fixed stars, his reason in its contemplative aspect with Saturn and in its social aspect with Jupiter, (and) as to his irrational part, the passionate nature with Mars, the eloquent with Mercury, the appetitive with Venus, the sensitive with the Sun and the vegetative with the Moon."*

One day I know scientists will be able to uncover the truth behind the roots of our souls and we will be left in awe. Maybe that is what the world needs - to truly understand that we are part of something beyond imaginable, and if we keep destroying our planet, we will only be hurting ourselves in the end. What will happen if we continue on this path of destruction and polluting of our earth? Will our seemingly eternal souls eventually die or are our souls imperishable? Osiris appears to have the metaphysical answer to that question.

> *"Can souls die?" asked Hermes. "Yes", replied the voice of Osiris, "many perish in the fatal descent. The soul is the daughter of heaven, and its journey is a test. If it loses the memory of its origin, in its unbridled love of matter, the divine spark which was in it and which might have become more brilliant than a star, returns to the ethereal region, a lifeless atom, and the soul disaggregates in the vortex of gross elements."*

Hermes Trismegistus
The Hermetica Wisdom Texts from 2nd Century AD

Such powerful words.

The three stars

References to stars as living and thinking souls can be found throughout our ancient history in many cultures. One of the most popular references are the Sanxing (deities) or also known as 'The Three Stars' (Fu, Lu, and Shou) found in Taoism and Chinese religion thought to date back to the Ming dynasty. It was during the 276-year ruling of the Empire of the Great Ming (1368-1644) that The Three Stars initially revealed themselves in human form. The three souls originating literally from the stars in our night's sky. In Chinese, San means three and Xing means star.

The Sanxing are comprised of the three elements thought to symbolize the good life:

1.   Fu - Prosperity, happiness and good fortune
2.   Lu - Status and respect
3.   Shou - Longevity and health

Almost always displayed in order from right to left, the Star of Fu represents Jupiter, the Star of Lu represents Ursa Majoris, and the Star of Shou represents Canopus (Carinae).

The Sanxing have remained so accepted and admired that you will find symbolic statues of Fu, Lu and Shou in literally millions of homes and businesses worldwide to this day. The awareness of stars embodying souls is so widespread it is the way of life. Taoist deities include humanizing planets and stars and believe the stars composing the Great Dipper also represent the cosmic bureaucracy of the gods.

See the stars shining bright

When we look up at the night's sky with the naked eye, we should be able to see approximately 3000 stars from the earth's vantage point. To us, the stars vary in brightness and some stars appear to shine much brighter than others. In terms of star brightness, many factors play a role including apparent magnitude (the appearance of brightness from earth), and absolute magnitude (the appearance of brightness from a standard distance of 10 parsecs or 32.6 light years and no loss of light due to absorption by space dust particles and gas). Luminosity (the amount of light energy produced by the star from its surface irrespective of its distance from earth) is also measured and should not be confused with brightness.

Reflecting our innate preoccupation with the stars can be validated through observing the ancient star maps of our pioneering astronomer ancestors. Star maps catalogue each star and trace the visual history of humanity's curiosity and desire for celestial guidance. The oldest known star charts are believed to date back to approximately 33,000 years ago. Evidence of cataloguing star brightness can also be found in ancient history in the work of Hipparchus of Nicaea, the Greek astronomer, mathematician and geographer, who worked in the 2nd century BC.

Imagine if all the stars in the sky were exactly alike. What if they all had the exact same composition, magnitude, luminosity and every single thing about them was the same? First off, we could possibly never see night if every star shone bright and were of great magnitude. They could all quite feasibly blend into one bright shining light with no differentiation, lose all their individual significance and we would ultimately lose all interest in looking up. The sky would lose that uniqueness that 'each grain of sand' concept brings, and eventually as time passed, we would potentially lose all purpose.

Individuality, seen within the concept of a greater whole, is what makes our universe great. We don't all have to shine with the same intensity. Our brightness is a matter of perspective. Our compositions are diverse. Our energy is constant. We all have a part to play and we all hold individual significance in the ebb and flow of life.

When you look up at the night's sky you will see stars of all colours, shapes and sizes. The skies are a reflection of humanity. We can naturally be drawn to certain stars, just like we are inherently drawn to certain people when we first meet them. Being different does not lessen the value. Most importantly, we are all capable of shining bright and increasing our energy levels of intensity in times when we need it most.

We are but just a speck of dust living on a grain of sand

So why exactly do we wish on stars? I believe we wish on stars because of their eternal significance. We are all ethereal beings that have a hunger for transcendence. We've always had, and always will have, a fascination with the stars and a fascination with wishing – both unknowns, both at the root of all creation. The stars are a source for inspiration and intellectual challenge. Just as stargazing involves looking for indirect clues to uncover the unseen, it is remarkable how much the concept of wish making does as well.

Invest some time into stargazing and you may find it will bring you closer to our universe. When you look up at the stars you will begin to realize just exactly how insignificant we really are in the grand scheme of things. The process of simply observing, taking it all in and increasing our sheer capacity to wonder allows us to contemplate on the unknown unknowns. Our earth is like a grain of sand in comparison to our universe, and we as humans are but just a speck of dust living on a grain of sand. It has been said that if we learn to master the starry heavens above and everything it contains, we will intuitively hold the key to our universe in the palm of our hands.

There are more than enough stars for each and every one of us to wish upon and each have our own. And remember, when you wish upon a star, it is the first step in making your dreams come true.

Know that when
you wish on a star,
someone, somewhere,
is wishing on it too.

SHOOTING STARS, SPACE JELLYFISH, KILONOVAS & MORE ...

Seeing a shooting star and making a wish is a ritual believed to have the power to grant wishes. This superstition dates back to the ancient world. Funny enough, shooting stars are not, in fact, stars at all. They are meteors, which are made up of pieces of interplanetary rocks or debris. When they break into earth's surface, they light up the night sky and leave a momentary trail behind.

Both day and night, millions of particles collide in our atmosphere but for obvious reasons we can only see them at night. Apparently, on any given night, a shooting star should be visible every 10-15 minutes and the number drastically increases with the captivating occurrence of meteor showers. Unfortunately, with all the light pollution we have in this world, potential for cloud cover, and the moon's ability to wash out the fainter ones determined by the moon phase, you may not see any at all. With that being said, depending on where you are in the world when you look up at the night's sky, the rarity of actually seeing a shooting star ultimately makes us feel like something special will happen.

We may not always be able to see shooting stars, so in their absence I still believe you should wish on the brightest or first star you see. But if you are determined to increase your odds of seeing a shooting star, you can search the internet for yearly meteor shower calendars (on average there are approximately 21 meteor showers per year with a peak period between August and December). There you will find a list of dates throughout the year listing the constellation meteor shower names. The names of each meteor shower are categorized based on the name of the constellation from which they appear to originate from. For example, the Perseid Meteor Shower appears to fall from the Perseus constellation. The Perseids are the most popular of the meteor showers as they can 'rain' typically between 50-200 meteors an hour! Once you have identified the best viewing times, try to situate yourself in the most optimal position for viewing and travel to the countryside or an area where there is reduced light pollution and you have unobstructed views. You will also need to get there a bit early to allow yourself enough time for your eyes to adjust to the dark (30 minutes on average should be enough time to boost your chances).

Shooting star legends

According to legends originating in Europe, it is believed if you make a wish upon a shooting star your wish will come true. In approximately AD 127-151, Ptolemy the Greek astronomer documented that shooting stars were actually stars that fell out of the gap, between the universe of the Gods and ours, when the Gods peered out from this gap to observe those here on earth. Ptolemy then furthered this claim by stating that if we on earth actually noticed these falling stars and simultaneously made a wish, the Gods would hear us as they were watching intently. Given the rare opportunity for this gap to be open, it would increase the chances for the Gods to both see and hear us. It was additionally interpreted that the Gods would grant wishes to all the individuals that made wishes at this time as they were most connected, observant, and have an incredible relationship with the universe and beyond.

Wishing on shooting stars, or fallen stars, became so widely believed it transformed to legendary prominence and continues to this day. In Chile, when you make a wish upon a shooting star, some believe you must also pick up a stone in the same moment. Meanwhile in the Philippines, rather than picking up a stone, you must tie a knot in your handkerchief instead.

However, not everyone in the world feels shooting stars are so lucky. Some Ancient Greeks related shooting or falling stars to falling human souls, and some of Jewish or Christian faith equated the falling stars to fallen angels and demons. Some let their imagination get the better of them and according to Aristophanes, a Greek playwright, he conjured up that shooting stars are the souls of impoverished people, walking home inebriated after they had dinner at an opulent star. No matter what you believe, simply looking up at the stars can bring out the creative essence of your soul.

Space jellyfish

When you are looking for shooting stars, it is a much longer process than wishing on the first star you see. You need to invest a great deal of your time to find that perfect moment to align yourself with nature in order to witness the spectacular, yet ephemeral, interplanetary event. Moreover, if you spent enough time looking up at the night's sky and familiarizing yourself with astronomy, you will begin to 'notice' more – not just the grandiose nature of it all on a whole, but the actual intimate details. You will learn to discover things you've never seen before, even though they may have always been there.

Just as rare as shooting stars, are the breathtaking systems of Space Jellyfish when clusters of galaxies collide. When an unfortunate spiral galaxy plummets into a galaxy cluster, the fiery gas shreds away the spiral's gas producing streamers giving birth to new stars. The streamers are blue in colour, representing the youngest stars, and leave a beautiful trail behind the galaxy cluster like tentacles of an actual jellyfish. Try to imagine the pure beauty of this miraculous event. Just as jellyfish float on ocean currents within their wonder in the far depths of our seas, Space Jellyfish also gracefully float within our night's sky. Everything within our universe has its own inner sea – InnSaei.

InnSaei is the sea within. InnSaei has a borderless nature that links to our inner compass of constantly moving thoughts, feelings and imagination. Not only is there a sea within our own souls, but our universe also holds its own sea within. Stars, planets, comets, galaxies and so much more all have their own paths – their own destinations. The universe is alive with energy. No wonder we are constantly drawn to the stars. If you are blessed to witness Space Jellyfish, embrace the moment and make a meaningful wish.

Kilonovas

Vast amounts of vital knowledge have been obtained from studying the stars. It's no wonder they are a source of continual fascination and are linked to wish making rituals. Every day new discoveries are being made. Someone, somewhere, is uncovering something new.

On August 17, 2017 a monumental astrophysical event occurred in the form of a kilonova. Scientists were able to witness two neutron stars crashing 130 million light years away. They crashed so hard they made our universe wobble and actually produced gold and platinum. Not only were scientists able to see the incredible blast through the ripples created in space-time, but they were able to 'hear' it as well.

The crash enabled scientists to answer several outstanding questions that have remained unanswered up until this point. Scientists now know what actually happens when two neutron stars merge. The colliding stars revealed that this is a source for the origin of heavy elements and the cause of short duration gamma-ray bursts. Humans are now able to detect gravitational waves and this occurrence will be the source of future research discoveries for the years ahead.

The result of the crash really is a perfect example of how the efforts of literally thousands of people, over the years, have contributed to the fulfillment of a theoretical concept becoming eventually validated. I can only imagine the feeling of all the scientists suddenly realizing that what was once just an idea, is actually real. Interestingly enough, all that was revealed from the crash was something thousands of individuals have been wishing for years; yet more than a century ago, Albert Einstein predicted it.

Why kilonovas? They will help you find the 'gold'. In order to create a kilonova and produce gold, or other alchemistic elements, two neutron stars need to collide at great intensity or a neutron star needs to merge with a black hole. How are they able to do this? The stars contain the base materials required to foster creation. In order to fulfill your wish and find your gold, you need to obtain the base materials as well. If certain elements are missing you may not achieve the desired results.

What is even more interesting about this particular recent event is that scientists claim that the crash caused our universe to wobble. What exactly does that mean? Creating a wobble in something means that there must be containment in order to experience it. If our universe has no containment how can that be? This impression of a wobble leads to the concept of containment on the whole. In order for our universe to be contained, something must exist outside that containment. Furthermore, if our universe is actually contained, then that means we are but just one of many.

Our universe has a natural frequency and I believe the more we tune into it, the more we will discover. Meditation, relaxation and intuition practices are just a few ways we can learn to tune into the earth's frequency, or as I like to call it, the earth's heartbeat. Once we are able to master these skills we will be able to make the connection to the foundation of life itself. I believe in the near future we will know exactly what exists beyond our universe, as we all know it.

I also believe we will have scientific confirmation that the power of wish making is definitely real. By using our own inner frequencies and tapping directly into the earth's consciousness, we will instinctively be able to directly influence our life paths and their outcomes on a grand scale beyond imaginable.

Stargazers

Stargazers are those who are fascinated with the heavens above and often gaze at the stars. As long as humans have populated the earth, stargazers have been in existence. Evidence of stargazers and examples of celestial iconic art have been found dating back to the Chalcolithic period, known as the Copper Age, between approximately 3000 to 2200 BC. This was a significant period in the development of human technology.

There are approximately fifteen of these Chalcolithic Stargazer idols still in existence in near complete form. They gained the term 'Stargazers' as they all have heads that are slightly tilted back with slender necks. On the whole, they are both sleek and abstract while very curious looking, and create the impression that they are gazing up looking at the stars - further confirmation of our human wonderment.

Get lost in the heavens

You can never get tired of our night's sky. The simple act of looking up at the stars every night and getting lost in all its splendour will leave you in awe. As long as I can remember, I've had a fascination with the stars and what lies beyond - the desire to understand the universe as a whole and how we all fit into the equation. After all these years, this feeling has never ceased. I know in my heart we have so much to uncover, so much to learn and discover. I am filled with eternal hope and never-ending dreams that one day, we will be able to both see and completely understand the true beauty of our existence.

I encourage you to look up into the night's sky and get lost in the heavens. The stars are waiting for your wishes. The stars are in your soul. Embrace every moment. You are part of such an incredibly fascinating universe that is constantly changing and evolving. There is no end.

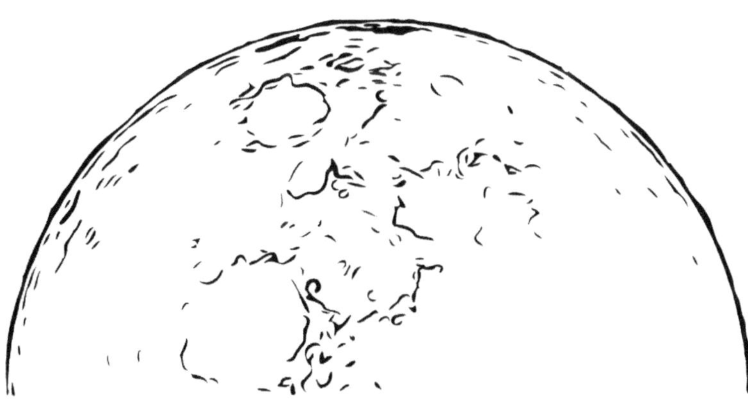

Fall in love with
the moon and everything
that appears to be
unreachable.

MOON RITUALS

Our fascination with astronomy

Our fascination with astronomy continues further into the realm of the unknown. Not only do we wish on stars and falling stars, but we also place value on other astronomical bodies, such as the moon. As with the sun, we similarly see the moon rise everyday, and we see it set. We are a unique species of curious explorers always seeking the new and continuing to thrive for more. I believe one can never get tired of looking up at the night's sky. How lucky are we to be able to look up every night and have a real, live personal observatory – a sea of diamonds and precious jewels.

Each day is a symbol of a new start, a new beginning. There is something peaceful about looking out into the sky every night before we go to sleep and think about the endless possibilities of what else may be out there for us. What lies ahead? Thoughts about whether there is more to life than meets the eye.

Humans have an innate curiosity for seeking life on other planets. We appear to be constantly searching for unique environmental signatures – footprints of civilizations gone by or even the present day footprints of extra-terrestrial life. What is the perceived pay off? Pure knowledge. And it is with this knowledge we believe we will understand the eternal questions of why we are here and what is our ultimate divine purpose?

Moon facts

Rather unique in its appearance to us here on earth, looking up at the moon is drastically different than looking up at the stars. Depending on the lunar cycle, the moon can be seen in different phases (or changing illumination from our perspective) displaying hues of various colours. On special occasions, we are also blessed with both hypnotic solar and lunar eclipses.

Following are some thought-provoking moon observations:

- Luna, Gaia, or simply Moon? Founded in 1919, The International Astronomical Union (IAU) was formed with the mission to "promote and safeguard the science of astronomy in all its aspects through international cooperation." Part of their responsibilities includes naming all objects outside of our earth's atmosphere. You may see the moon referred to as several other names but the official approved name is actually Moon.

- The origin of the moon is still a mystery. Scientists have developed theories regarding its creation but none have been confirmed. The most probable theory states the moon is actually accumulated space debris caused by a Mars-sized body colliding with the earth.

- It is conventional belief that the moon has always had virtually no atmosphere, yet in recent years scientists are making great discoveries about the moon. In October 2017, NASA research indicates the moon did indeed have a short-term substantial atmosphere approximately 70 millions years ago consisting of carbon monoxide, sulphur, and water.

- Just as the moon affects tides here on earth, the mystery remains regarding the moon affecting our sleep patterns. I always know when it is a full moon without even looking up at the night's sky. My body has an intuitive internal clock tied to the moon phases. More concrete research needs to be investigated regarding lunar rhythms and sleep patterns, but nevertheless, the notion is incredibly intriguing.

Life on the moon?

What lies beyond the boundaries of our earth, as we know it? We have come to the realization that there must be more. Throughout the world we continue to see epic structures emulating constellations and other planets within our universe on our very own planet earth. When we try to scrutinize photos of the moon, some people believe they are able to clearly see similar epic structures and other phenomenon that appear to be on its surface. This leads to the rise of questions that fuel curiosities. Was the moon once inhabited? The lack of high quality photos leaves the question open to interpretation. The answers may remain unanswered but our fascination with the moon endures.

The man in the moon

Due to the moon's synchronous rotation with the earth, the moon always shows the same face (or hemisphere). Amongst the many craters that cover the moon's surface, moon gazers believe the moon appears to have a face looking down on us – often referred to as 'the Man in the Moon'. The Man in the Moon has inspired stories for generations and the image varies depending on the pareidolic interpretations or patterns seen in the random highlands and lunar maria.

The Man in the Moon has become associated with helping you sleep and enabling good dreams for the new day ahead. Legend has it that he will assist you in bringing you peace while you sleep.

When you go to bed at night, it is the best time for clarity, setting intentions, releasing your wishes, and laying the groundwork for positive dreams and night visions. It is a time to clear out all the clutter from your mind that accumulated during the day, and allowing your body to rest and regenerate for tomorrow, free from any 'noise'.

Other images can also be seen on the face of the moon. According to East Asian mythology, the Moon Rabbit (also known as the White Hare) can be seen mixing a potion. The Moon Rabbit is believed to be making the elixir of immortality providing humans with eternal life.

Full moon wishes

Moonlight inspired festivals, full moon parties, full moon and new moon wishing, mooncakes and food offerings to honour the moon, and more, are all part of ancient traditions originating from moon worshipping and gazing. In many ancient cultures it is believed that the moon brings great power to the earth and humanity. Wishing upon the moon is associated with gratitude, letting go, transformation, abundance, and allowing your mind and soul to be open and receive what is to come.

Many cultures today remain fascinated with the moon's cycle. These lunar phases have inspired the creation of associating the moon phases to different human characteristics and desires depending on the phase. For example, the most popular time for wishing upon the moon is the new moon phase. The new moon is associated with new beginnings, creation and rebirth. It is the best time to wish if you desire to embark upon something new in your life and to inspire you to wish for your ultimate heart's desire.

The first quarter phase is associated with assembly and building, and is the best time for wishing for drive and momentum.

The full moon phase is when the moon is believed to emit its greatest power. If you are struggling with something, this is the best time to make your wishes for assistance in overcoming struggles and any impedance. Full moon blessings take away bad luck and misfortune and bring renewed hope and good fortune.

The last quarter phase is associated with a time for reflection and review. This is the best time to contemplate your previous efforts and wish for assistance in guidance, optimism, and preparation for the next new phase.

Wishing on the moon is similar to wishing on a star. Simply close your eyes and make your wish when the timing is right. Being the closest of the heavenly bodies to earth, the moon is awe-inspiring and holds such great presence. It's no wonder we naturally want to wish on it and draw upon its powers. From a new moon, blue moon, to supermoon, you can always wish upon the moon and ever changing appearance caused by changing illumination from our perspective along with its proximity to earth. Embrace the captivating powers of the moon and elevate your wish into a transcendent experience.

The lantern festival & the first full moon

Diverse in its origin, the Lantern Festival is commonly known as a traditional Chinese festival. In the past, the customs, along with the celebration times, differ depending on the various cultural legends ranging from Taoism to Buddhist legend, the era of the Qin Dynasty, and more. Regardless of origin, the concept itself has the widespread theme of being connected to the new moon, the deities of our heavenly skies controlling the destiny of humanity, and the celebration of good fortune by sending wishes into the sky.

Today, the Lantern Festival is an integral part of Chinese New Year celebrations. It typically occurs on the fifteenth day of the month in the lunar calendar marking the first full moon of the Chinese New Year and is also the final day of the Chinese New Year festivities. The festival is notorious for attracting large crowds and is a great example of widespread faith and belief in the power of wishing. The festival gained its name by literally the use of placing paper lanterns outside homes and businesses (on the eve of the Spring Festival) and launching sky lanterns later into the night's sky full of wishes for the Lantern Festival.

Over time, the lanterns have become much more elaborate and can be seen in a variety of colours, designs, shapes, sizes, and colours. Each lantern released represents its own special wish. For instance, a white lantern represents a wish for good health and successful beginnings, a red lantern represents a wish for good fortune and love, an orange lantern represents a wish for wealth and success, while a light blue lantern represents the anticipation that your wish will come true. The lanterns are then further personalized by writing or painting specific, personal wishes onto them before they are released.

Common wishes to write on your lantern include:

- All wishes come true - 心想事成 (xīn xiǎng shì chén)
- Things will happen as you wish - 事事如意、心想事成
  (shì shì rúyì, xīn xiǎng shì chéng)

Different versions of the Lantern Festival have been celebrated worldwide for centuries from China, to Thailand, India, Portugal and Brazil, to name just a few. During the Lantern Festival in Thailand, the releasing of the sky lanterns represent the releasing of bad luck. However, in conjunction, people also make wishes on flower lanterns (made of banana leaves and flower blooms decorated with candles and joss sticks) and release them into the river for good luck.

Sky lanterns are used year round for several other occasions and special celebrations throughout the world. The Chinese New Year Lantern Festival and other festivals alike, all demonstrate the tremendous value that people actually place on wishes. Festivities centred on sky lanterns symbolize the whole concept of wish making and confidently setting intentions to be released to our heavenly skies above.

A word of caution regarding releasing sky lanterns – you must understand that the lanterns do pose extreme environmental hazards, fire hazards, along with several others risks such as the interference with aircraft navigation and more. Some countries have banned their use including both manufacturing and possession. For all of these reasons and beyond, it would be best to choose an alternate wishing ritual that does not negatively affect the environment around us or rather than launch sky lantern, keep it somewhere meaningful.

Energy & connections

Uncovering the origin of making a wish upon the moon remains a mystery and is difficult to pinpoint. Nevertheless, the existence of rituals demonstrates just how many different cultures link wish making to celestial bodies. Prior to all the technological inventions that readily connect us to each other today, humans relied on nature, including gazing at the celestial bodies above, for guidance. Reliance on the seemingly elusive powers of gods and goddesses, energy and connections, and recognition for receiving extrasensory information from our natural world quite possibly provided more faith and confidence in wish making in the past, above and beyond what we see today.

There are countless reasons why humans have always felt a strong connection to the moon. The way it lights up the night's sky reminds us that it is, by far, the most dominant celestial body in such close proximity to us. So many things around our world today are linked to the moon and all its wonder. From the construction of epic structures and the alignment with many of the wonders of our world, such as the full moon and its relationship with Stonehenge as an icon of early astronomy, to the belief the moon is sacred as validated by Poya in Sri Lanka, the moon holds great perceived power and significance in our everyday lives.

Our world is so immense and we have so much to learn. Technology and research are moving at an ever-increasing pace that it is proving almost difficult to keep up at times. With that in mind, I would encourage you to spend time to learn as much as you can about our historical past to understand where we have come from. The more you research our ancient history, the more you will discover. It is important to familiarize yourself with some of our earlier traditions and rituals, for there you will find proof that our connection to nature and the world around us is inherent to our souls and genetic makeup.

The secret is part of us - we just need to harness its great powers.

Wishes hold
special magic.

FOUNTAINS & WELLS

The importance of water

Water is life. And without water there is no life. Water gives life, sustains life, and has a natural ebb and flow. It is a symbol of immortality. It is a sacred gift. We need to bless water and appreciate it. The water we have here on earth has been here since all creation and we cannot love it enough. Water is one of the many beautiful gifts from Mother Nature that teaches us how to love. It can teach us how to nurture and appreciate the simple, yet essential, good things in life.

Water is sacred. If you live in a community that appears to have endless supplies of clean drinking water, you are tremendously blessed. If you live in a community that has limited access to clean water, or none at all, you will more than likely be in tune with the fact that water is a sacred gift. It is due to the insatiable need of humanity to desire more and more material objects and the lack of care and apathy for our beautiful planet that we have polluted all our natural water resources. All the indigenous cultures of our world shared the belief that water is sacred. At what point did some cultures shift and have what appears to be a disregard for this gift?

The world has shifted. All the nature patterns and rhythms are changing and have been disrupted by humanity. Technology and desire fuel the incessant drive for wanting more, but at what cost? Here we are, now with scientists and researchers looking for other planets in our universe that may be able to sustain life as we are on a constant path of destruction here on earth. And what might be one of the key factors that these scientists are looking for? Water. That's right. Water on other planets. Water that is needed to sustain life. Why has the search begun to look for other planets that we can potentially live on rather than focus on 'fixing' the very incredible giving planet we live on today? What are humans lacking inside that drives the masses to lose all respect for the planet that relentlessly gives?

Water lust

We take water for granted. We are water lust. We need water to nurture us, bathe us, and clean our 'things'. We need it to feed our plants and animals, to provide a habitat for a host of hundreds of thousands (and quite possibly the steady decrease of millions) of sea creatures and plant life, to regulate the earth's temperature, and a host of countless other factors. We use water for our own personal enjoyment, to travel on with boats, to swim in, and spiritually to provide us with a sense of calm. We touch it, we feel it, we drink it, and we listen to it. But worst of all, we pollute it.

It is our responsibility as inhabitants of earth, to change what has been done and reverse the damage now. We are now at a point, which is blatantly obvious, that we need to heal our planet and give back to Mother Nature before it's too late. Remarkably fascinating, the question always arises, why don't we create new water?

Historically we have not created water scientifically because the process of mixing, and ultimately linking, hydrogen and oxygen is highly dangerous and we wouldn't be able to create water on a large enough scale that is required to sustain our worldwide population. However, the quest to create it appears to be on the upcoming horizon. But more importantly, why would we even fathom creating water when it is most abundant and plentiful right here, right now? Wouldn't the most logical approach be to preserve and conserve what we have available to us already? One would think so.

Water facts

We are dependent on nature for survival – physically, intellectually, emotionally, and intuitively. Water is a connector and connects us to everyone and everything in our universe.

Following are some thought-provoking water observations:

- Water is an irreplaceable molecule responsible for the creation and sustenance of life here on earth.

- Water covers approximately more than 70% of the earth's surface. Water is a source of inspiration for finding life on other planets.

- According to the National Oceanic and Atmospheric Administration, as of July 2018, more than 80% of our waters are still awaiting human exploration and also remains unmapped and unobserved.

- From outer space our earth has the appearance of a tiny blue marble due to the abundance of water. The Apollo 17 took an iconic (but not the first) image of our beautiful earth on December 7, 1972 giving rise to the name "The Blue Marble" amidst a sea of environmental concern with the frailty of our planet.

- At birth, the human body is approximately 75-78% water and as we age that percentage can drop to an average of roughly 55-60%, however there is a constant of around 75-80% water in our brain no matter our age. Water lives in our bodies providing assistance in the insulation of our organs, distributes essential nutrients, flushes out toxins, enhances mental development, and so much more. Water allows life to thrive and supports all living organisms.

- Water bends all the rules and chemists love it for its enigmatic qualities. Water is a source of energy and a superior solvent. More things dissolve in water than any other solvent. Water freezes, melts, and floats (ice). It is a rare substance that has the ability to float on itself when frozen.

- Water is one of the four classical elements: Water, Earth, Air, and Fire.

Fountains & wishing wells

Water has special significance and the gift of water has been observed since the creation of life in all indigenous cultures, societies and religions worldwide. The scarcity of clean water provides a significant challenge to our very existence. Wherever clean water could be found, monuments were constructed to contain and protect the water. Creations of water fountains celebrate the gift of water, while creations of water wells house the sacred water.

The concept of water being interconnected with spirituality and sanctity is forever embedded into our lives. Ancient cultures believed the gods protected these shrines and wells that contained precious water. Fountains and wells became symbols of spiritual monuments where people could come and express not only gratitude for water, but also to make personal wishes in the presence of the gods. These blessing rituals would contribute in making the wishes come true.

Bestowing small tokens of appreciation or offerings, and linked to good fortune, it became customary that people would make a wish on a coin then gently toss it into the fountain or well. It is interesting to note that the value of the coin does not need to correspond with the perceived value of the wish. This wishing ritual became so popular that these spiritual monuments became widely known as literally wishing fountains and wishing wells. While its origins are still unknown, it is believed it dates back to European folklore.

Today, it is nearly impossible to find a fountain or well without coins in them. Even with undetermined origins, and its worshipping connection lost, many people feel wishing wells and fountains are nostalgic reminders of their childhood.

I encourage you to use your nostalgic feelings to reinvigorate your belief and fuel your inspiration to take action and fulfill your innermost wishes. Return to those childhood memories where you once believed anything was possible. Indispensable power can be drawn upon from embracing a youthful mindset.

As a matter of conservation, I would add a note that unless a body of water or fountain is a dedicated wishing monument or wishing well in a public place, please refrain from throwing any coins into the water. The coins are a proven deadly hazard for marine life. If you feel inclined to make a wish, simply make your wish without tossing a coin and your reward will be even greater.

Weave your visions into
the fabric of your soul.

BRIDGES

Bridges make destinations once thought to be unreachable, reachable. They connect point A to point B whereby creating a direct path, yet allowing for continued passage below. They assist in overcoming physical obstacles, make connections, and are designed to provide passage for people, animals or things. They answer the symbolic question,"How do I get from here to there?"

Differences in bridges demonstrate differences in visions and ultimately create different experiences. Throughout the world we see bridges made of rope, steel, concrete, wood, and stone, to name a few. There are different types of construction, each with different weight loads and different purposes.

Some are purely functional, while some are architecturally pleasing to the eye. Some are simply famous and iconic like the famed London Bridge in the United Kingdom, the remarkable Golden Gate Bridge in San Francisco, the transparent Zhangjiajie Glass Bridge in China, the tallest by structure the Millau Viaduct in France, one of the longest suspension bridges Akashi Kaikyo Bridge in Japan, the longest pedestrian bridge the Charles Kuonen Suspension Bridge in Switzerland, and the list goes on.

Wishing over & under bridges

Finding the origin of wish making in correlation to bridges has proven to be most challenging. One thing we do know is the approximate timeline for the construction of bridges. So logically any wish making rituals would have to relatively correspond to the time period of when construction of bridges began as an utmost starting point or at some point thereafter.

The Guinness World Records claims the oldest datable bridge still in use is the bridge over the Meles River in Izmir, Turkey dating from c. 850 BC. Mycanae, Greece also hosts a number of other fragmented bridges over the Havos River dating from c. 1600 BC and on.

The connection to the gods can been seen in both rivers in ancient mythology and legends. Meles was a river god and the father of the poet Homer, while references to the name Mycanae can be found in its earliest written form in the works of Homer. Theoretically, wishing rituals in relation to bridges could quite possibly be linked to this timeframe known for the worshipping of gods. The symbolic nature of a bridge crossing over a river god could naturally have been a source of inspiration for wishing and bring good fortune.

When it comes to actual wishing rituals and bridges there are several versions depending on the origin. These rituals represent how diverse our world can be, yet still unifies us with one concept - wishing.

Following are some wish making rituals for bridges:

- **Pont Marie Bridge in Paris**
  a.k.a. The Lover's Bridge, where tradition has it that when you are on a boat and travel underneath the bridge, you are to kiss the person next to you and make a wish and it will come true.

- **Overpass in Fengyuan District, Taiwan**
  a.k.a. The 'Wish Lock' Bridge, where a more recently created wishing ritual that began in approximately 2004, has turned into a local phenomenon. People write their wishes on padlocks and attach the locks to the wire fence on the overpass.

  It is believed that the trains that pass below the bridge create a magnetic field and an abundance of energy that accumulates inside the locks to release and fulfill the wishes contained within.

- **Ioannovsky and Bankovsky Bridges in St. Petersburg**
  In the 18th and 19th centuries several floods afflicted St. Petersburg. After restoration of the Ioannovsky Bridge in 2003, sculptor V. Petrovichev erected a metal sculpture of a startled hare on top of a wooden post in the water that specifies heights of past major floods. The monument represents a hare that saved his life during a flood by jumping into the boot of Peter the Great. Onlookers are supposed to make a wish and throw a coin at the base of the hare's feet to have their wish fulfilled.

Similarly, if you rub the head or paws of the golden winged lions of Bank Bridge and make a wish, the lions will use their spiritual powers to make your wish come true. In St. Petersburg you will find many other wishing monuments as well.

- **Charles Bridge in Prague**
In 1683, exactly 300 years to the day marking the anniversary of the death of priest St. John of Nepomuk, his statue was erected on the bridge that led to the castle. Although this statue is but one of many located on the bridge, his statue in particular, is widely known as a wishing statue. The archbishop declared him a martyr and his statue symbolizes his honour for never revealing the Queen's confessions to King Wenceslas IV, but paid with the price of his life. St John was executed and his body was thrown over the Charles Bridge into the river below. When he drowned, five stars appeared in the water highlighting the circle of stars found on the actual statue.

In order to have your wish fulfilled, you need to touch the falling priest on the shiny portion of the plaque on the right hand side and make your wish. This wish making ritual is so popular that the actual shiny portion of the plaque turned a golden colour due to the amount of people that have literally touched that spot while making a wish! No one knows exactly when the wishing legend began, however it is quite common when paying respect to someone who has passed, to touch a part of the memorial or marker in hopes of implicitly connecting on a higher level.

- **The Wishing Bridge in Old Jaffa, Israel**
Literally named The Wishing Bridge, visitors come to Old Jaffa seeking this short bridge. The bridge has a large plaque with the inscription "An ancient legend holds that anyone boarding the bridge, holds its zodiac sign and looks at the sea – their wish will come true." The wooden bridge overlooking the Mediterranean Sea contains on its railings twelve bronze plaques – one for each of the twelve zodiac signs. This area of Old Jaffa contains many references to astrology including the infamous Zodiac alleys – a network of alleys all with zodiac sign street names.

- **The Wishing Bridge in The Gap of Dunloe, Ireland**
  Another bridge named literally for its meaning. The Gap of Dunloe is a narrow mountain pass that dates back two million years. The gap was created by the Killarney's Ice Age when the snow and ice thrust through the Killarney Valley. The tiny stone bridge is located between the scenic Coosaun Lough and Black Lake. It is believed if you make a wish when you cross over this bridge, your wish will come true.

  The Gap of Dunloe and surrounding region is a haven for geological treasures and rare plant species. This unique spot has a definite earthly connection deeply rooted with Mother Nature. It is no wonder the bridge is identified with the spiritual network and wishing.

- **Bridge of Sighs (Puente de los Suspiros) in Lima, Peru**
  The bridge was originally built in 1876, and rebuilt two years later after it was destroyed in the War of the Pacific in 1881. An important landmark for the Barranco region, the wooden bridge is linked to a story of heartbreak.

  There is a legendary story of a young woman, born to a wealthy father, who forbids her to be with the man she loves – a street sweeper. The young woman would gaze out her window in despair, longing to be with her soul mate. Passers by on the bridge would literally hear her sighs and thus the bridge gained its iconic name, The Bridge of Sighs.

  Legend has it that you are supposed to hold your breath the entire length of the 30-metre bridge, and if you are able to make it to the other side in one breath, you are to make a wish. Wishes made upon this bridge are destined to come true.

Making unreachable places reachable

There are so many bridges associated with wishing rituals all over the entire world. I believe the reason they continue to hold such wonder and allure today is due to their truly symbolic nature of making once thought unreachable places to be reachable with ease, and the joining of two domains.

Bridges represent life's constant changes of leaving behind your comfort zone and what is familiar, and crossing into the unknown. Getting to the other side of a bridge may present itself initially as a mystery, however, a bridge is a symbol of not only hope, but also progress. Sometimes when we get to the other side, we may just find what we are looking for. So next time you cross a physical bridge, take a moment, clear your mind and a make a wish.

This may be your
best adventure yet.

RAILROAD TRACKS

The 17th, 18th, and 19th centuries were significant time periods for the transportation industry and industrialization. It was in the 19th century where railroads drastically changed technology and the essence of the railway journey. Trains were literally making dreams come true. Trains became the new lifelines connecting cities, transporting not only goods and supplies, but also people, whereby fulfilling essential travel needs opening up doors for new opportunities. Railroads and locomotives quickly became icons of progress displaying dominance over our landscapes and a pivotal point in human culture.

To a conductor of a train, railroad tracks hold clarity and there is a clear path, specified destination and purpose. To onlookers, many cross its tracks on a regular basis but may not know where the tracks lead or where exactly each train is headed. It is this reason in particular, that gave birth to the numerous metaphors that have been formed regarding railroad tracks. These metaphors are beautiful representations for optimistic views on life. Many people may cross our own paths throughout our lives, and not all will know or understand what our personal destinations may be at the time. We are the conductors of our own trains and we hold our future in our own hands. People board and deboard our trains, yet we control our ultimate destinies.

Trains are guided by railroad tracks and are known to blaze trails through a variety of cities and backdrops symbolizing what we as humans long for. Connecting wish making and railroad tracks is a natural synergy, where innovative technology interconnects with cultural change opening a new world for human desire. It was in this 19th century timeframe when uniting railroad tracks and wishing took hold when the hidden connections between the two became characteristically apparent.

Crossing railroad tracks

This old folklore varies, but if you make a wish while lifting your feet as you drive over railroad tracks, it is supposed to bring you good luck and the hopes that your wish will come true. Crossing over the tracks symbolize desire, progress and new opportunities. I remember throughout my childhood, sitting in the back seat of our car and my Dad driving over railroad tracks. Immediately he would remind us to lift our feet, raise our hands over our heads, close our eyes, and make a wish. He always wanted us to be reminded that we could achieve anything we desired.

To this day I am forever wishing on railroad tracks – with the exception of keeping my eyes open if I am the one driving! This wishing ritual holds great nostalgia and fond childhood memories for many.

Railroad bridges

For those just starting out in hopes of pursuing their dreams, the combination of railroad tracks and bridges is like a twofold wish epitomizing the pathway yet to come. When you are a passenger on a train and the train passes over a railroad bridge, you are to make a wish and remain silent until the train reaches the other end of the bridge. If you do so, it is believed your wish will come true.

Walking on abandoned railroad tracks & rails to trails

For those with legal access to allow you to walk on abandoned tracks, if you are able to walk the rail for the length of 16 ties without falling off, and you make a wish prior to doing so, your wish is thought to be destined to come true.

Train tracks are filled with metaphors. The allure of not knowing where the tracks lead and an unwritten future hold great curiosity. To some it is a great place to make wishes; to others it's a great place to take photos. Unfortunately, it has become a dangerous viral trend and numerous people have died in the process of being on the tracks. The interest in railroad tracks comes with a huge warning and it is an extremely hazardous activity if the tracks are live and still in use. Railroad engineers say there is absolutely no safe way to be on a railroad track period. Judging the speed of a train is next to impossible and an approaching train is almost silent as the sound of a train follows behind it. If a conductor sees something on the track and pulls the emergency brake, it can take more than 1-2 minutes for the train to come to a complete stop equivalent to the length of approximately 18 football fields. For all these reasons alone and many more, no one should ever tempt fate and walk on railroad tracks that are still in use. There are so many other ways to make wishes and I urge you make your wishes in the safest manner possible.

As newer forms of transportation emerge, the nostalgia and romance we once had for the original railways diminish. In fact, many past railroad tracks have been abandoned. Fortunately through organizations such as Rails to Trails in the United States, is the realization that these unused rails can be used for the emergence of new trails, eloquently combining the past visions of railroad track symbolism with new trails. Same trails, same optimistic connotations, same wishing concepts – just simply transformed by using the unchanged wishing undertones we've always had in the past.

We are all a link in the chain

We all hold a special place in the universe no matter how big or small we may think our role is. We are all a link in the chain, a wave in the ocean, or a tie in the railroad. We are all part of something much bigger, much more intricate than we can even fathom. Fortunately, we have been blessed with the ability to allow ourselves to draw upon this special hidden connection by tapping in, praying, or simply wishing. Believe in your heart with the purest intentions, and you will unlock the wealth you've been searching for.

Make a wish.
Make it magnificent.
Make it happen.

BIRTHDAY CANDLES

A birthday is a celebration for the gift of life that commonly includes cake, candles, the gathering of souls, a birthday song and wishes – fulfilling all our **Four Classical Elements of Mother Nature:**

- **Earth:** The creation of cakes, baked goods and food – all made by harvesting the bounties of Mother Nature's earth. Mother Nature is most generous and holds the key to our well-being and a healthy life.

- **Fire:** The tiny flame from each lit candle representing the eternal flame, the power of fire, and fertility of the divine.

- **Water:** The gathering of souls. Overall, we are all made of a high percentage of water. Without water there is no life. Water is at the root of all creation. A birthday celebrates the gift of life.

- **Air:** Symbolic in more ways than one. Birthday celebrations allow us to feel the joy in the air. It is the presence of souls and connecting with the breath of life. The air we create by singing songs in celebration bringing our souls closer together. We also create wind by blowing out the candles after making a wish and allow the air to carry our wishes forward.

Plus one more – **The Fifth Element:**

- **Aether:** The act of making a wish and sending it out to the universe to be received by the heavens above. The element of the spirit or quintessence – the material between our terrestrial and celestial realms.

Why is it that every year for our birthdays we celebrate with the popular tradition of putting candles on a cake, closing our eyes and making a silent wish? When celebrating a birthday, we traditionally put one candle on a cake for every year that we are here on earth. Then we take a moment to close our eyes, silently put great thoughts out in the form of a wish for the new year ahead, and blow out the flames from the candles – all in a single breath. If you are able to blow out all the flames in one breath, your wish will be granted. All along we are taught not to share our wish with others, as we are told it won't come true if we do. Out-dated myths leave us with forever imprinted and preconceived notions that if we reveal our wish to others, it will never be granted. In essence, we jinx our wish.

Now pause. Take a moment to think about it – every year we look forward to blowing out those candles. We revert back to those fond childhood memories of actually making a wish in hopes for it to come true. Reflect back to the time when you've just finished making your wish and blown out your candles. As soon as you are done, all that is in our presence is birthday cheer and anticipations of your wishes coming true. The celebrations continue and you are filled with renewed hope and belief. What would happen if you revealed your wish? Would the party be over? What would the reaction be of those attending your celebration? Would people encourage you to follow your dreams and feel fortunate to be amongst a group of people whom you shared your personal thoughts and wishes? Or would their first instinct be to let you know that now you have shared your wish, it won't come true?

Wishing has a way of making our innermost desires come to the forefront. Our birthday celebrations are yearly reminders of the necessity to make wishes, pursue what you are most interested in, and follow your purpose in life. It is easy to make a wish on your birthday then quickly move on to the next thing. If you don't create a plan to mirror that wish, you may let a whole year go by without making it actually happen. Then when it's our next birthday, we do the same thing all over again. Rinse and repeat.

Wishes tend to bring out the best in all of us. Wishes can be a catalyst to bring positive change to all of our lives and hope for a brighter future for not only us, but also generations to come.

One of the seven wonders of the world - The Artemesium
It has been said that the origin of putting candles on baked goods dates back to Ancient Greek times and is directly related to one of the Seven Wonders of the World, the Artemesium.

The Artemesium, also known as the Temple of Artemis is located in Ephesus - modern Turkey. The temple was constructed in mid sixth century BCE to honour the Greek goddess of the Moon and the Hunt, Artemis. With varying construction and design elements not entirely typical of that time, it is believed that various gods were also worshipped in this temple including The Mountain Mother or Great Mother - Goddess Cybele. Cybele incorporates strong aspects of the Earth Mother Gaia and Harvest Mother Demeter. Statues could be found in the temple symbolizing fertility, and the earliest temple contained a sacred stone believed to be a fallen meteorite from the planet Jupiter.

Visitors of varying backgrounds and beliefs would come to the temple bringing baked goods beautified with lit candles in hopes of praying to the gods and making their wishes come true. The lit candles with the flames represented the glow of the moon, the power of fire and the light of life. Blowing out the candles releases your wish into the universe and the smoke that forms from blowing out the flames aid in carrying your wish to the gods.

Ironically, the Artemesium temple was destroyed by its first fire in 356BCE on the same day Alexander the Great was born – his birthday.

The calendar year

Early references to blowing out candles can also be traced to 18th century traditions in Germany known as Kinderfest, and can similarly be found in numerous other cultures. Over the years, the concept of baked goods and candles evolved to become part of our present day birthday traditions that include celebrations with guests not only bearing good wishes, but gifts as well. Blowing out candles on a birthday symbolizes the anniversary of a birth, a rite of passage, and the hopes that all the wishes will come true for the individual who is celebrating. The number of candles adorned on the cake typically represents the age of the celebrant.

The calendar year is a significant marker for most. When we think of our own personal life, we think of it in terms of our age or number of years we have lived and yet to live. The years denote various stages and in turn, our accomplishments. Birthdays are gentle reminders that time has passed, will continue to pass, and allows for the simple reflection of our life's journey and purpose. It has been said that no one should have a birthday without blowing out a candle and making a wish.

Think back to your previous birthday wishes. What kinds of things do you wish for on your birthday? Typically every wish we make has a core of truth and a desire to will it to come true. Tune in to your birthday wishes and make them part of your reality. Develop a plan to make it happen. There are no wishes too small or too big. As long as your intentions are pure, and if you have the drive, desire and determination, the odds are in your favour.

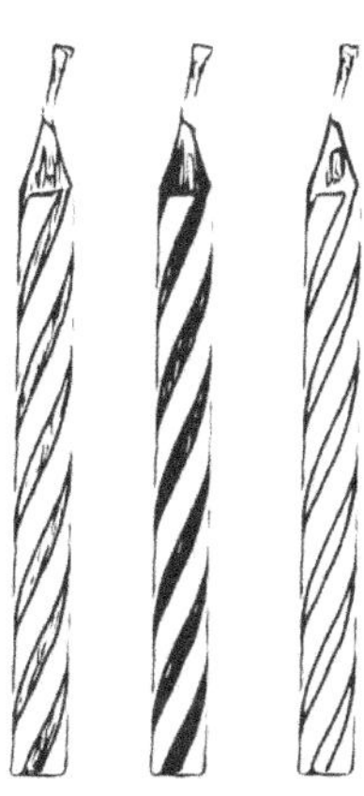

I made a wish
for you.

THE WISHING HOUR 11:11

History has it that when you see 11:11 on a clock you are to close your eyes and make a wish. The origin of the Wishing Hour has been around for generations yet its conception is unknown.

The number 1
The number 1 plays a significant role in many aspects of our lives including science, mathematics, religion, philosophy, technology, and more. From a Mathematician's perspective, the number 1 is a leading number and the first physical number.

By definition, 1 is often referred to as unity, represents a single entity and is the probability of an event that is anticipated to take place. In technology, 1's and 0's are used in binary code and the number 1 represents the flow of electricity meaning 'on'. 1 is the leading number for the Fibonacci Sequence with related patterns occurring repeatedly in biological structures and closely related to The Golden Ratio.

The insight into mathematics runs deep and can unveil hidden concepts within our universe - for behind mathematics lies formulas, patterns, structures, rhythms, regularities, and a whole different perspective for analyzing anything and everything. Essentially, mathematics enables us in understanding the essence of all matter and the world that we live in.

In numerology, the number 1 holds great significance in our universe. It is often referred to as the origin of creation and a primal force that embodies spiritual symbolism. It is associated with new beginnings, synchronicity and oneness. That in turn is tied to the belief in divination, enlightenment, the presence of a collective soul and meaningful coincidences.

The origin of creation - Building blocks

Let's begin with the number 1 as it relates to the notion of creation. Number 1 is the most basic building block. In Mother Nature, cells are the most basic building blocks and all living organisms on earth are composed of at least one cell. At least one cell must be present in order for life, as we know it, to exist. Now think of the same concept but with 1 wish. At least one wish must be present in order for an idea, as we know it, to exist.

Conceptualize the presence of cells in our human bodies with making 1 wish. Every cell appears to be both small and simple, yet each is programmed to complete a variety of different tasks either independently or together with others. Our bodies have so many different cells that all work together in unison and continually divide to also grow and make repairs in the process. The human body is continually replacing old cells with new ones at an overwhelming rate of millions per second.

The whole concept is mind-boggling. Wishes are just like cells. When one wish is created and fulfilled, it then continually grows and can be refined. Each wish can work either alone or with others in order to be fulfilled, all with different tasks. And like all cells, wishes too can expire and either be replaced or permanently retired.

Performance & science

So many aspects within our history can be related to the number 1. A great deal of emphasis is placed on the fact that everything starts with the number 1 or it only takes one to begin, trigger, break the ice or lead the way. Regarding performance, whether academic, athletic or other, '#1' represents being the best in class, excellence, dominance, and conveys the image of confidence and leadership.

The number 1 is significant in the world of conventional science whereby there is a belief that before life there was nothing (0) and everything was created from one explosion. In it's simplest of forms, the Big Bang Theory is a predominant explanation of how our universe began with a small primordial singularity. The theory claims the universe began with an infinitely small point and expanded out from there. Once again we are seeing the notion of creation linked to the number 1.

Philosophy & religion

In philosophy, the number 1 is a symbolic representation of 'The One'. According to the philosopher Plotinus (204-270CE), who is regarded as the founder of Neoplatonism, he believed in three major principles: The One, The Intellect, and The Soul. Plotinus proposes that The One is the transcendent Creator, the source of all existence, and the higher being of absolute unity. The One is the eternally present possibility beyond all scope of being and non-being, and that we all ultimately share one mind.

Plotinus laid the groundwork for spiritual cosmology. His work outlined that The One is all-inclusive, encompassing all that exists – all that we see is one and The One is love, light, the divine, and ultimately the Infinite Creator. He contemplates that the soul is neither the body nor dependent on the body, and the mind plays an active role in shaping its experience rather than a passive role of perception.

Plotinus' work also incorporates happiness (the human good) and the measures for attaining it. The One is present in all, both nothing and everything. It is always there for those who embrace it, are prepared for it, and are ready to receive it and draw upon it. We can only gain knowledge of The One through experience and manifestation.

I believe The One represents eternal possibility and is directly in line with making all that appears seemingly impossible, possible – hence it all starts with 1 wish.

According to Philo of Alexandria (20BC-AD50), who is considered to be the founder of religious philosophy, both the letter and the number system holds great value in interpreting the Hebrew Bible. He believed that the number 1 is God's number to seek deeper meaning into the Bible otherwise known as gematria.

Astro-numerology

As declared by Galileo Galilei (1564-1642), *"The book of nature is written in the language of mathematics"*. Galileo's theory on this concept can be found in the early revolutionary book The Assayer published in Rome in 1623. Mathematics and numbers can be used to decipher many things in our universe and hold numerical significance rather than chaotic coincidence.

Pythagoras of Samos (c.1570BC-c.495BC) is an influential contributor to both philosophy and religion. He believed numbers, especially the number 1, are the root of God descending into matter, rulers of ideas and divine macrocosm. Proficient in the Law of Vibration, Pythagoras claimed that every number has a particular vibration and believed that there is no education that will guide humans more through spiritual evolution than through the knowledge of spiritual mathematics.

Pythagoras claimed that odd numbers are feminine and even numbers are masculine. The odd numbers relate to certain qualities that are spiritual, intuitive, artistic, emotional and inspirational. The even numbers relate to qualities that are analytical, skeptical, self-reliant, physical and materialistic. Pythagoras believed consciousness is in everything, including numbers.

Tying Pythagoras' beliefs together with astrology, we see the creation of astro-numerology, the union of the science of our universe with the science of numbers. In astro-numerology each of the nine numbers correlate to the nine planets of our solar system. The number 1 represents the Sun, the luminary Ravi, of which all remaining of these planets orbit around.

The number 1 holds a meaningful place in astro-numerology and indicates new beginnings, spiritual revolution, and may even control our destiny. It symbolizes simplicity and the transformation of life in a positive manner. Ironically, the numerology horoscope also indicates that if your personal life path number is 1, you will be determined to accomplish all of your unfinished tasks. Furthermore, you will be provided with both the determination and inspiration to transform your wishes, hopes and dreams into reality.

Feng shui & Chinese culture

The number 1 is simple yet has the most multifarious cultural meaning in Chinese culture. In Feng Shui, Taoism and general Chinese culture, we once again we see reoccurring themes of new beginnings, creation, unity, unobstructed flow, and more.

The number 1 is believed to affect everything from your professional life to romance, and even the meaning of the numbers on your house or floors on an elevator. It is considered to be a lucky number and according to several Chinese philosophers, *the mother of all creatures*. It brings success, victory, leadership and influential qualities, and can lead to prosperity.

The magic of the number 11

Not only is the number 1 considered to be a formidable number, but in its double-digit form, the number 11 is considered a Master Number in the Chaldean or Pythagorean system. Master Numbers are deemed to possess more potential than any other numbers. The Master Number 11 is the most intuitive number, is regarded as a channel to the subconscious, the master of light and a spiritual messenger. It is also linked to achievement, faith, innovation and inventions, being a visionary and having psychic abilities.

Overall, the Master Number 11 is the dreamer. And to be a dreamer, one must have the potential for an elevated degree for learning, realization and achievement in any type of environment. No matter how difficult to handle or how inconceivable the dream may be, you must recognize that it requires time, effort and maturity. Once you have achieved your dream you can become a Master Teacher and share your learnings with others. With this theory you can see a high correlation of how The Wishing Hour 11:11 may have come to light.

The meaning of 11:11

The Wishing Hour 11:11 is related to so many facets of our lives and can be seen in mathematics, science, philosophy, religion, and more. Together in repetition, the numbers 1 and 11 represent new beginnings, synchronicity, originality, oneness and the divine. Through numerology and the analysis of numbers and their influence on human life, societies all over the world that utilize number systems and spiritual mathematics, are able to gain a deeper understanding of our universe and the mystical realm.

Throughout history, it has been said that when you see 11:11 you should make a wish and it will come true. 11:11 also comes twice a day making it twice as likely for your wish to come true. It is widely believed that the potential for wish fulfillment becomes enhanced at this particular time. With the numbers 1 and 11 having so many references to creation, superior beings and mysterious origins, it may also be when the divine window opens up and the paramount time when the spiritual world communicating with us is heightened.

I believe it is a great opportunity for you to pause, be in the moment, create intention and manifest your thoughts. If you are one of the lucky individuals who repeatedly sees 1's and multiples of 1's, you are having direct contact with your angels, guardian angels, spiritual guardians, and celestial energies. The resonance of this number has numerical significance and is connected to synchronicity and oneness. As best affirmed by the famous psychologist Carl Jung, *"Synchronicity is an ever present reality for those that have eyes to see"*.

The number 1 has undoubtedly held spiritual mathematical importance throughout time. The number 1 in sequence or repetition claims 11:11 will bring the best of luck. Remember to stop and pay attention to your surroundings when you see 11:11 to assist in understanding its meaning. It is believed that if you truly comprehend the number 1, enlightenment is yours. With the many meanings behind the number 1, we can only believe that 11:11 is truly The Wishing Hour and a perfect time to magnify your wishes. So the next time you see 11:11, close your eyes and make a wish.

Other compelling numbers

Prefer another number or time of day? 1:11? 2:22? 3:33? 4:44? Brilliant. There are no rules. There are no absolutes. If you feel drawn to another number, make it your own. As long as it holds personal significance and provides you with a little reminder of your wish, then you are on the right path.

IMAGINE PEACE

احلم سلام (Arabic)

想像世界有了和平 (Chinese)

ILARAWAN ANG MUNDONG MAPAYAPA (Filipino)

KUVITTELE RAUHA (Finnish)

IMAGINEZ LA PAIX (French)

წარმოიდგინეთ მშვიდობა (Georgian)

STELL DIR VOR ES IST FRIEDEN (German)

חלום שלום (Hebrew)

शान्ति की कल्पना करें (Hindi)

KÉPZELD EL A BÉKÉT (Hungarian)

HUGSA SÉR FRIÐ (Icelandic)

ᓴᐃᒻᒪᖃᑎᒌᓂᖅ (Inukitut)

IMMAGINA LA PACE (Italian)

平和な世界を想像してごらん (Japanese)

평화를 꿈꾸자 (Korean)

به صلح بیندیش (Persian)

IMAGINA A PAZ (Portuguese)

ПРЕДСТАВЬТЕ СЕБЕ МИР (Russian)

IMAGINA LA PAZ (Spanish)

TUFIKIRIENI AMANI (Swahili)

சமாதானத்தை நினையுங்கள் (Tamil)

ཞི་བ་སྐྱོམས (Tibetan)

BARIŞI DÜŞLE (Turkish)

SPIRITUAL &
SACRED PLACES

Visiting spiritual places and monuments are perfect locations to make your innermost wishes and release them to the universe. Many feel the unexplainable powers of hidden nature may manifest itself in these sacred places. If you place yourself in the midst of such intangible powers, it is believed you can tap into these powers and magnetize your wish towards you through The Law of Attraction.

Sacred places are plentiful and located worldwide. If you have a specific type of wish, it may be worth aligning yourself to the place that best matches your wish.

Imagine peace

Do you have a wish that will bring peace and possibly make the world a better place? Try seeking out places that hold significant meaning in your local community. Or better yet, the next time you are travelling, plan in advance and research your destination for any special monuments or locations. After making your wish in this type of memorable environment, when you return home, not only will you feel good, but you may also have a great story to tell.

There are many monuments all over the world dedicated to peace that hold great presence and meaning. The Imagine Peace Tower is one of my favourites (from afar as I yet to visit but it is on my wish list). Located on the tiny Videy Island in Reykjavik, Iceland is the iconic memorial from Yoko Ono to her late husband, John Lennon. The monument is based on a wishing well design with several interior lights that combine together to form the perfect single beam that illuminates the sky above in such a magnificent way. The words 'Imagine Peace' are inscribed on the monument's exterior native Icelandic stone face walls in 24 different languages.

Yoko Ono came up with the original concept in 1965, however it only became in final completion and first lit on October 9th 2007 at the unveiling ceremony, in memory of John Lennon's birthday. To add to the sheer beauty of the Imagine Peace Tower, is the addition of over one million wishes from all over the world that are buried in the ground surrounding the monument. The beam of light itself is meant to express all the wishes to the universe. I would encourage you to view the original unveiling ceremony online and send in your own wishes. If you would like to visit the site in person the dates the tower is lit up is also available online.

Kumano Sanzan & Kumano Kodo pilgrimage routes & Meiji Shrine
There are several locations worldwide that are likened to being 'almost heaven' or the 'land of happiness'. Places so rich in spirit and thriving with good energies that one cannot help but notice. The Kumano Sanzan, made up of three holy sites, in Japan is one of these special locations. These areas are considered to be sacred since ancient history. During the 9th-12th centuries, these shrines became particularly popular leading the way for future generations to observe and respect the beauties held within.

The prevalence of wishing can also be connected to the Kumano Sanzan. If you are looking to make a wish while you are there, Kumano Nachi Taisha Shrine is the spot. In order to get there, you need to walk the extraordinary long cobble stone stairway, called the Daimon-zaka, lined with beautiful trees and bamboo groves. Located on the surrounding premises of the shrine is Tainai Kuguri. Tainai Kuguri is a highly regarded sanctuary symbolic of rebirth, purity of the soul and the divine. To make a wish, you must bring a Gomagi (pieces of wood for the gods) inscribed with your wish through the hollow root of the nearby camphor tree and your wish will be destined to come true.

Large camphor trees make for great wishing trees. Meiji Jingu Shrine in Tokyo is also another notable location where you can write your prayers and wishes on Ema (little wooden tablets) and hang them around a large camphor tree. In addition to writing an Ema, you can also write a Kiganbun, (a letter to the deities) expressing your gratitude or wishes along with an offering in an envelope. The Meiji Jingu Shrine is an area dedicated to worshipping and wishing, and if you are looking to spread your luck, you can wish on a coin or receive Omikuji (pre-printed fortunes) to hang on the nearby wire fences.

Stonehenge

If you are fascinated by our never ending universe and what lies beyond, and are always wishing on stars, you may be interested in visiting one of the great wonders of our world. Another sacred, yet inspiring location to make your wish experience more thought provoking is Stonehenge in England. Widely recognized for its megalithic stone structures, Stonehenge represents the raw strength and power of ancient civilizations and is an incredible example of achievement. The first early henge monument was built approximately 5000 years ago, with the iconic stone circle erected circa 2500 BC. Who built it remains a mystery. Its purpose? Another mystery.

People visit Stonehenge for a variety of reasons, primarily for the significance of its architecture, sacred geometry, burial site and the enabling of scholars to understand ancient ceremonial practices. However, I also believe it is a brilliant place to go to if you are looking for inspiration and a chance to connect on a different level. With diverse theories on its origin and purpose, the most common are related to astronomical observation. Theorists claim it was once used as a mechanism to predict eclipses, solar events, and times when earth energy cycles were most influenced by the moon, sun and stars – an astronomical calendar. In more recent times, with evidence of injuries and illness found in some uncovered human remains, the site is believed to be associated with supernatural healing linked to the possible powers of the stones.

The fact that the site still remains a mystery is alluring in itself. I couldn't think of a better place to increase your motivation, set your intentions, take in the hidden energies and feel connected to our past. Take note that thousands of people visit every year. If you are feeling lucky, you can try to obtain one of the limited special stone circle access visits in advance. Designed specifically for a much smaller group to view the stones up close, this will make your visit much more personal and meaningful.

These examples are just but a few of the numerous locations in the world that are believed to be sacred where spiritual essences are heightened. Research locations that best suit you, and take your wish to a whole new level by including incredible experiences that mirror your innermost desires.

Wishing chairs

Along with spiritual and sacred places are wishing monuments. Wishing monuments come in all shapes and sizes, and you can even find 'wishing chairs'. Believe it or not, there are actually several wishing chairs in the world, and two of the most notable natural stone ones, are located in Ireland.

On the northern coast of Ireland, you will find the most extraordinary rock formations that will leave you in awe called the Giant's Causeway. Local legend tells quite an interesting story and claims they are the work of a former giant Finn McCool (a.k.a. Finn mac Cumhaill). Geologists have attempted to come up with more rational explanations regarding their origin and claim they are formed from volcanic activity more than 60 million years ago. However, I believe their octagonal shape and stepping stone puzzle formation is not quite so random as the result of violent volcanic eruptions. There are over 40,000 basalt, interlocking columns! This leads me to contemplate that their origin is still awaiting to be discovered and will continue to remain a mystery for a very long time.

At the site, located within the uniquely shaped pillars of rocks you will find the legendary "The Wishing Chair". Legend has it that you must wiggle four times before sitting on the stone chair. Once you are seated, put your hand on the left stone, close your eyes and make your wish while rubbing the stone with your left hand. If you make your wish in the correct manner, it is said that your wish will be fulfilled.

Another popular wishing chair is also located in Ireland, in Bundoran at the Fairy Bridges at Tullan Strand. Rumour has it that this wishing chair marks the grave of Chieftain O'Flaithbheartach. In order to make a wish on this chair and have it realized, you must also follow some legendary guidelines. Before sitting in the wishing chair, your approach must be gentle and gradual as not to disrupt the great powers the chair holds within. Once you are seated, you are to take in all your surroundings and express gratitude for Mother Nature's splendour, and also for those who may have sat in the chair before you. Your wish must be genuine, with good intention, and made in silence. Once you have made your wish and you are ready to get up from the chair, tap the seat twice for additional good fortune.

When angels are near,
feathers appear.

FEATHERS

Feathers – made of protein keratin, often adorned with brilliant colours or patterns, so intricate in design, yet light and beautiful to touch. Feathers have a delicate appearance, but they are extremely strong by nature enabling flight while keeping the body warm and protected. The feathers of vertebrates are extremely complex and phenomenal integumentary structures (the integumentary system is the organ system including the skin, feathers, hairs, and more that covers the body and protects if from external damage). Feathers are a natural wonder of structural engineering and biology.

Dating back to ancient times, humans have developed a fascination with feathers. Feathers encapsulate one of the countless splendors within our world. When you look at a feather up close and see all of the beauty contained within such a small yet unassuming object, you begin to realize just how complex and scientifically sophisticated our world really is. And when you begin to contemplate on whatever or whoever ultimately designed and created everything we know today, you begin to understand the exceptional attention to detail and complexity of it all and how everything is truly interconnected. So much detail and biological entanglement contained within one tiny fragment of our existence.

It is easy to fall into the trap of taking our world for granted. How often do you stop and truly take in everything around you? Have you ever stopped to pick up a feather and look at it – really closely and in detail? Learn to be more aware of your surroundings. Notice things. Notice fallen feathers. They are inconspicuous gifts from the birds, or as some would say, *"When angels are near, feathers appear"*. Throughout history, feathers have been symbols for angels and wishing. It has been said that when angels are present they are there to hear your prayers and assist in carrying out your wishes, hence, the link of feathers to wish making rituals.

Feathers are symbolic connections to freedom of flight, purity, creation and transcendence. They are synonymous with the soul. Native Americans idolize feathers, and the gift of a Golden or Bald Eagle feather is of highest reward for its spiritual significance connecting its owner to the 'Creator'. Ancient Celtic Druids wore robes adorned with feathers in elaborate ceremonies designed to summon the gods and connect on the ethereal plane.

Feathers were also of great significance to the Ancient Egyptians. The Goddess Maat was notorious for her *"Weighing of the Heart"* ceremony where she would weigh the hearts of the dead against her sole *"Feather of Maat"*. Hearts that were lighter or of equal weight to the feather indicated a life of virtue and their souls would continue the journey to Aaru – reed fields, commonly known as an Egyptian paradise or eternal heaven.

Next time, when you come across a feather, you will effortlessly tune in to knowing what it means. Proceed to concentrate on the feather, close your eyes and make your wish. As legend has it, the angels will hear your wish and assist in making it come true.

An alternative way to make your wish is to draw a picture of the fallen feather on a piece of paper and also write your wish on the paper asking the angels to bless it. Wishes with pure intentions will be granted. Keep this paper somewhere significant and use it as a reminder to take action in making your dreams come true.

As with all things, make sure you investigate local laws on any of your wish making rituals. Picking up feathers can be illegal in some countries. For example, the 1918 Migratory Bird Treaty Act of the United States and Canada makes it illegal to possess feathers of migratory birds amongst other things. Other countries have also since joined this act.

Every raindrop is an
opportunity to wish.
Let it rain.

RAINDROPS & RAINBOWS

Raindrops

Through the existence of all humanity, is the knowledge of the eternal importance of water. In the form of raindrops, rain provides our landscapes with the necessary nourishment for the birth and sustenance of the fruits of nature. And with the lack of water in so many parts of our world throughout history, its absence is what re-emphasizes and reminds us of its perpetual significance. Without rain, indispensable landscapes can be drastically altered affecting entire ecosystems.

The presence of rain has countless benefits for all life on earth. In addition to providing all our plants and fauna with essential nourishment, it is the main source of fresh water supply replenishment deposits on our beautiful planet. Rainfall can be used as an energy source, influence ocean currents and in turn influence our weather systems. Monsoons are known to have the ability of radically changing barren landscapes into lush, vital ecosystems. Early Indian healers used rainwater to treat illnesses. Even the sound of rainwater is believed to open up the heart chakra. These are just but a few examples. The benefits of rainfall appear to be endless.

According to early Hinduism and ancient sacred writings, rainfall was connected to the gods above. The iconic Indra, the King of Gods (heaven and divine) and also of rain, thunder, lightening, and river flows, was a Vedic deity in Hinduism. He was worshipped for his powers in destroying all evil and deceptive forces, including those who obstructed happiness and abundance to those on earth. Rainfall and its associated phenomenon was the gods' form of communication with those on earth. Blessings came in the form of raindrops. Making wishes on raindrops was a form of communication for humans to respond directly to the gods. Still today, Hindus practice ancient Varuna Yajna, the practice of worshipping The Gods of Rain. Humans have consistently had a natural affinity for rain as validated by all the various symbolic rain rituals found worldwide throughout our history.

Watching the rain fall can be cathartic. It's like the sky is cleansing itself, releasing the impurities and washing them all away. And with the rain, comes new life and nourishment, healing of the soul. Walking in the rain and allowing it to pour upon your body and drench your clothes through to your skin is both liberating and therapeutic. It can make you feel at one with nature. The sights, the sounds and the textures are hypnotizing. On a side note – if you do decide to get wet in the rain, make sure you are able to quickly find shelter and get warm so as to not affect your health. And also avoid any lightning or thunderstorms!

If you are one who does not like to go out in the rain, but rather stay indoors, it can be a great opportunity for you to observe the great powers that rain can possess. It is from within your protected shelter you will also be able to make your wish upon the raindrops. When the rain falls against the window, look for a single raindrop on the glass. As it falls down the windowpane, make your wish before it intersects with another raindrop and your wish will be fulfilled.

Rainbows
Wishing on raindrops is connected to rainbows. As the general saying goes, *"Without raindrops, there are no rainbows"*. Another form of wishing relating to raindrops is that of wishing on rainbows. Similar to that of most wish making rituals, wishing on rainbows is perceived to be in existence for thousands of years, yet its origin is difficult to determine.

Rainbows are often indications that the rains have passed. Rainbows are a natural phenomenon and appear when there is a combination of two essential weather elements: sunshine and raindrops. Rainbows can vary in size, length and intensity depending on many factors, including individual perception. On occasion you may even be able to see a rainbow with two arcs (secondary, multiple or even twinned). On the rare and extraordinary occasion, you may be blessed to witness a full circle rainbow.

Your own pot of gold

Many people also wonder if you can see the end of a rainbow. The majority of scientists claim it is not possible. I am letting you know it is possible. I have been fortunate enough to see the end of a rainbow years ago in Niagara Falls, Canada. I didn't go chasing it mind you. It actually came to me while I was standing reminiscing with some very special people. We all saw the end of the rainbow meet the ground right before our eyes within approximately 15 feet from where we were standing.

The experience was completely breathtaking and surreal. And just in case you were wondering, there were no leprechauns or physical pot of gold at its base! However, the fact that I was able to actually be in the presence and witness the end of a rainbow itself was my own personal pot of gold. I will never forget that feeling and will be forever grateful for that extraordinary experience.

Remember, the only way you to find the end of your rainbow is to get outside and explore the world around you.

Wish upon a rainbow

There are a variety of wish making rainbow rituals that can be made. Most popular being, when you see a rainbow, you are to close your eyes and make your wish, and when you open you eyes at the end of wishing, if the rainbow is still visible, it is believed that your wish will come true.

Wishes hold
great powers when
we set them free.

WHITE HORSES

Blazing a trail

The most distant ancestor of the horse dates back to approximately 55 million years ago. In historic times, horses were wild and often hunted. Evidence of domestication of horses is believed to be around 5000BCE but still open to debate and not definitive.

Horse domestication and human transformation of the world go hand in hand. Horses are responsible for playing a foremost role in creating significant change for our advancement. Horses greatly assisted in agriculture, communication, transportation, power generation, and so much more. It is the only mammal whose contribution stimulated human progress on such an immense level and literally assisted in blazing a trail.

Wings, horns, strength & beauty

White horses are particularly symbolic in worldwide mythologies. Some horses were depicted with wings such as Pegasus, while other versions include having a horn such as the infamous unicorn. White horses were believed to possess great powers and often used by the gods and goddesses.

Ancient images of white horses illustrate them as powerful and strong, yet beautiful and majestic. The Celts believed white horses were representations of the deities. It is ancient widespread belief that the most sacred horses are white. White horses are unique reminders encouraging the pursuit of your dreams.

The unicorn

The unicorn – a white horse with a single, spiral pointed horn, prominently protruding from its forehead. Fact or fiction? Are unicorns real? One thing for certain, these robust and striking beings have been in existence in stories, folklore, mythology, sacred texts, art and more since antiquity. Many accounts of this most wondrous creature are so detailed in description and convincing in nature, that one would tend to believe that they are indeed part of our world's natural history.

These mysterious and elusive, beautiful creatures are symbols of purity and strength. They represent perseverance and the motivation to never succumb to surrendering your will. Maybe that is why unicorns are 'uncatchable'. They are constant epitomes of the need to chase your dreams and to always push forward. If you are an optimist, unicorns are ubiquitous.

Modern day references to unicorns include the identification of a start up company valued at over $1 billion as a 'unicorn'. I would tend to agree with that correlation. Anyone who is been capable of starting out with just one wish, staying true to their course and pursuing their dream to that of such significance is not only unique and uncatchable, but incredibly inspiring. The unicorn acts as a reminder that all it takes is 1 wish to change not only your life, but those around you as well.

Pure & Divine

Seeing a white horse has such diverse symbolic meanings. In some cultures, white horses are associated with purity, the divine, and represent the balance of wisdom and power. Horses in general are widely accepted as representations of freedom of our spirits, or souls, free of any restraints and limitations. Horses are further linked to motivation, drive and having a strong inner strength.

It is believed that when you see a white horse you are to quickly make a wish prior to seeing its tail. If you are successful in doing so, your wish will be granted.

Make a wish ...

Snowflakes are
fallen kisses
from the skies above.
Make a wish.

SNOWFLAKES

Snowflakes are single ice crystals. They are individually unique with intricate shapes and patterns, and when they are of necessary size, they fall from the sky collectively as snow. In order to witness the sheer beauty of each individual snowflake, you must view them under a microscope or as macro-photographic images.

Snowflakes symbolize winter, purity, and uniqueness. When you are on the path to a new destination and looking for new opportunities, falling snowflakes are also symbolic reminders that in order to move forward you need to additionally let go.

Snowflakes and the image of angels seem to go hand in hand. Snowflakes are often believed to be kisses from angels in the skies above, sent as reminders for us to believe in the power of wishing. When snowflakes fall in abundance, they fall together to the earth and form in unison representing a white blanket - a clean slate, a new chapter, a renewal and opportunity for a new start. Making snow angels in freshly laid snow is also a common childhood memory for many who live in, or have experienced, colder climates.

It has been said that if you make a wish on the first falling snowflake of the season, your wish will be fulfilled. Better yet, wish on the first falling snowflake you see, no matter the occasion, to increase your odds. Other versions of this wishing tradition include wishing on the first snowflake that lands on your hand. If you make the wish before the snowflake melts, your wish will come true.

Me,
you,
& 2 blades of grass.

BLADES OF GRASS

Human connectivity to nature is of utmost importance. If we lose all connections to Mother Nature, we begin to take her for granted. Everything in our planet is connected. There is a constant ebb and flow, a push and pull affect that needs to be nurtured. Grass is a perfect example. Should you attempt to alter an area of grass, you cannot help but affect the whole. Its root systems are deeply anchored, contain fibrous networks, and regulate whole plant growth. Grass is both versatile and adaptable, and is an abundant valuable source of food and energy for other life forms in addition to raw materials.

Blades of grass are never found growing on their own - they are always together and surrounded by other blades of grass representing togetherness. This wishing ritual is to be made with a friend.

Pick two random blades of grass and place them in one of your hands in the form of an upright fist, with the uppermost tips of the grass sticking out only. You are both to close your eyes and silently make your wishes.

When you are both finished wishing, open your eyes and the person who is not holding the grass must choose one. It is believed that the person with the longer blade of grass will have their wish fulfilled. If both blades of grass are equal in size, both wishes will come to fruition.

Sometimes on the way
to fulfilling a wish
you get lost and
find a better one.

LEAVES

Leaves are symbols of growth and fertility throughout many cultures worldwide. Providing the breath of life, the leaves on the symbolic Trees of Life collect strength and nourishment, and when the leaves fall, their lives transform into providing the necessary food and nutrients for subsequent life. The leaves themselves are all unique in colour, shape, and size – not much different than humanity.

And with the Autumn Equinox, we are reminded of the influential stimulus that Mother Nature has on our everyday lives. When we begin to see falling leaves, we realize it is the ending of a past season, and the beginning of a new one. We automatically adjust to the changes and prepare for the coming of winter. Much like our own lives.

Harmony & balance
On a thought-provoking note, during an equinox, both day and night are roughly equal in length. This occurrence is considered to be a representation of both harmony and balance.

So the next time you see the autumn leaves gently falling, remind yourself that this may be an ideal time to release your wishes to the universe, not only with hope for them to be fulfilled, but to also bring harmony and balance to your life.

It is believed that if you make a wish on a falling leaf and you catch it before it touches the ground, your wish will come true. Should you decide to take your leaf home with you, make sure you preserve it well. Taking extra care of your wishing leaf may assist in the cultivating of your wish.

Four leaf clover

The four leaf clover is a rare find. The odds of you actually finding one is like winning the lottery and is highly dependent on the landscape and environment of which you find yourself in. Although some may not believe four leaf clovers are real, I can tell you from personal experience that they are indeed real. I have found them on more than one occasion, and have even once found a rather large patch of four leaf clovers in a field very close to where I live.

Each leaf of the four leaf clover is said to represent different meanings:
1. Faith
2. Love
3. Hope
4. Luck

The origins of good fortune related to a four leaf clover date back to Adam and Eve in the Bible when they were both cast out of the Garden of Eden. Before leaving Eden, it is said that Eve picked a four leaf clover to bring with her as a reminder of their time in Paradise.

The four leaf clover is also popular in Irish culture, and the good fortune that it brings dates back to the Celtic Druid priests with earliest references dating back to 4th century BCE. The Druid priests were highly regarded as religious leaders and often used four leaf clovers for both worshipping and healing rituals to ward off any evil.

Should you find a four leaf clover, pluck the stem, then close your eyes and make your wish. Be sure to keep your four leaf clover in a safe place as it is believed to be a good luck charm and it will continue to bring you good fortune while in your possession.

Sage leaves

Salvia - Latin for sage a.k.a. The Wisdom Herb. Sage is widely known for its medicinal properties and is associated spiritually with prolonged life and immortality, healing and protection, clarity and wisdom. The ancient ritual of burning sage is said to purify and cleanse people, objects or spaces from negative energies.

It is believed that if you write your wish on a sage leaf, place it under your pillow, and if you dream about your wish for three consecutive days, your wish will come to fruition.

Bay leaves

Another common form of wishing on leaves is through the use of dried bay leaves. Bay leaves, known for their distinct flavour and aroma, are often used in culinary dishes and stews. The leaves themselves are not meant to be eaten, but rather to be used for flavouring during the cooking process.

The bay leaf is thought to be a symbol for psychic connections, whereby the fragrance it emits when burned, opens up one's ability to engage in prophetic visions. Exact origins of wish making rituals and bay leaves are unknown, however, it is believed that if you write your wish on a dried bay leaf and burn it, your wish will come true.

Never underestimate
the power of a wish.

ACORNS

In line with all the previous symbolic references to creation, fertility, immortality, Mother Nature and its prevalent forces, are various wishing rituals relating to acorns from an oak tree. The oak tree itself is iconic for its depiction of impressive strength, purity, and immense planetary wisdom.

The Celts believed oak trees characterized the ability of humanity to overcome all odds and bestow great acts of kindness to all. The acorn is the seed of an oak tree and depicts both the creation of life and eternal life along with abundance and fertility. The acorn itself is the younger version of the mature oak tree representing life potential.

In numerous North American indigenous cultures, Ancient Greece and Iberia, and even throughout the Jomon period in Japanese early history circa 14,000-300BCE, acorns were a vital and reliable source of food for many. It is only natural that wishing rituals dating back to ancient times are linked with the mighty oak tree and its acorns.

Should you ever pass under an oak tree and have an acorn fall within your sight (or by chance, on your head!) – pick the acorn up, turn around three times, then make a wish and it will be fated to come true. Keeping the acorn in your pocket is said to bring you further good luck.

Your Isaac Newton Moment – when the conditions are right, acorns can literally rain down on your head. You may either end up in an emergency room or by chance be blessed with your own invention similar to that of Isaac Newton, the falling apple, Principia Mathematica, and the Law of Universal Gravitation!

Pure intention,
gratitude,
and wishes.
Our roots remain as one.

WISHING TREES & JARS

Wishing trees

The worshipping of trees is one of the earliest traditions in India. In Hindu mythology, the Kalpavriksha is known as an actual 'Wish Fulfilling Tree' and is cited in early ancient works. The concept of wishing on trees remains timeless. Wishing trees come into their own naturally. They are unique, distinguishable, and have a special quality about them that makes them stand out. I encourage you to research images of some of our world's most incredible looking trees. You will be left in awe.

Some captivating examples of mesmerizing trees include the Rainbow Eucalyptus typically found in the Pacific Islands, the flowering Wisteria trees in Japan, the giant Baobabs of Africa, the Dragon's Blood trees in Socotra, the towering Sequoia trees in California, the odd shaped Monkey Puzzle trees in Chile, and the Moreton Bay Fig trees in Australia. The numbers of miraculous looking trees are countless. The magic of trees and the perceived powers and energies within remind us of the interconnectivity of our entire universe and immortality. The shapes, colours and unique textures of trees can often be a source of inspiration to many.

Trees & inspiration

Lush nature, ancient pine forests, and magical landscapes combined with mysterious myths and legends often lay the foundation for creativity and the desire to think beyond and make the seemingly impossible, possible. Scotland is just but one of many places in the world where stunning landscapes make the backdrop for allowing your imagination to roam free. One of the most iconic representations of this can be found on Eilean Shona in Northern Scotland where J.M. Barrie was thought to be inspired to write the infamous Peter Pan and the ghost story Mary Rose.

The island is known for one of the most diverse Pinetum's in all of Europe, its panoramic views, rocky terrain, lush green carpets of moss, uniquely shaped trees, inlets, coves, spectacular beach at Shoe Bay, and so much more. It's an island known for hosting creative retreats and embodies J.M. Barrie's concept of never wanting to grow old. Guests are free to explore the entire island and even visit the Town Hall to paint a wish on a wishing stone and place it somewhere on the island for others to find. It truly is Neverland.

Wishing tree sites

Actual outdoor wishing tree sites can be found all over the world. People flock to these sacred sanctuaries to make their wishes. Being in the presence of such natural grandeur, those who wish are filled with faith and the hope that their wishes will be fulfilled.

Following are a few examples of outdoor wishing tree rituals:

- In much of Ireland, England and Scotland, you may find several wishing trees (a.k.a. fairy trees and clootie trees) covered with ribbons. People make a wish and tie a ribbon on the tree in hopes for their wishes to come true. Wishing trees located near wishing wells are more common and will be adorned with wishes throughout the entire year. You will also find coin trees where trees are literally filled with wishing coins that have been hammered into the tree trunks.

- Thailand has its own version of worshipping tree deities. Nang Ta-khian is the legendary female spirit known to inhabit the Ta-khian tree. Her spirit is accredited for enabling miracles and often you will find the sacred trees adorned with offerings and shrines.

- The two Wishing Trees of Lam Tsuen remain ever popular in Hong Kong. It is believed the trees have spiritual powers to grant wishes. Historically, people would come and write their wishes on joss paper, tie it to an orange, and toss it into the trees. The higher the branch, the more the probability for the wish to be fulfilled. Today, many people make wishes by tying the joss paper to surrounding racks and ornamental trees.

Wishing jars & indoor wishing trees

A more recent phenomenon that has emerged is the creation of wishing jars and indoor wishing trees. Wishes written down are believed to have tenure and are more likely to come true. Since they are written down and stored, they are quick and easy reminders of your desire to fulfill them. Written wishes can be kept in your own special storage vessel or simply hung from an ornamental-type tree within your home or work place. This new concept of creating your own version lets you bring your wish making rituals from the outdoor to the indoor.

Wishing jars or trees assist in prioritizing your wishes and allow you to readily share your wishes with someone else at any given point in time. Creating a wishing jar or tree can be a personal endeavour or with a combined group of wishes of family, friends, or colleagues. Wishes are to be kept and at the end of a year or specified period, you are to count how many have come true. It's a great way to record all your wishes in a creative manner to keep you inspired.

Your wish is
my command.

GENIE IN A BOTTLE

Legends, fairy tales, fairies, genies, buddhas & more

Wish making rituals appear to have been in existence since the creation of humanity – it is part of our souls, our makeup, and our creative essence. Wishing is connected to faith, belief, and heightens our fascination with all that is unknown, the creation of life itself and the spiritual evolution.

Wishing is a root cause for major technological advances that can be seen throughout the history of our universe. If humanity was not infatuated with moving forward, chartering new territories, and fulfilling our dreams, life would remain static.

Wishes are catalysts for making the seemingly impossible, possible. With that being said, it is only natural to cultivate wish making rituals and develop repeated subtle reminders and integrate them into our everyday lives.

In addition to the most popular wish making rituals already previously mentioned, references to making wishes can be seen in everything from fairy tales, genies in bottles, ladybugs and ladybirds, eyelashes, Buddha bellies, and so much more. Lists of wish making rituals appear to be endless. And the one thing they all have in common is putting your innermost desires out there to the universe and asking for guided assistance in making them become realities.

Genie in a bottle

One of the most whimsical views of wish making, and common in fairy tales, is the releasing of a genie in confinement. The origin of the nefarious genies, or jinn, can be dated back to approximately 2400 BC. Similar to humans, yet possessing great supernatural powers, the jinn lived intimately with nature and could change their appearance at will. Cheeky by nature, and the often the cause of great havoc in their communities, the jinn were eventually abolished and dispersed in the winds by the great gods. Only a few remain locked up in bottles or ancient oil lamps. Should one stumble upon one of these bottles or lamps, you are advised to exercise great caution and contemplation prior to releasing the genie.

Common ways to release a genie include uncorking of a bottle or by rubbing an old lantern, ultimately causing a genie to appear who will grant you three wishes. However, the wishes also come with restrictions: wishes for infinite wishes, ill will, or forced love will not be granted.

Quite often the third and final wish comes with great indecision. The one who is wishing places an inordinate amount on pressure on themselves, as they know that this is their last wish and it must be the 'right' wish to fulfill all their needs. The symbolic stories of genies in bottles or lanterns often highlight the ego of humanity and the insatiable desires for materialistic things. Wishing for pure personal gain, in the absence of potential negative impacts and caring for the world around them, may eventually open up the door for great heartache and consequences.

Depending on the nature of the previous two wishes, quite often the third wish will be used to undo the problems caused by the first two wishes. In the end, the most rewarding benefit is a moral lesson learned relating to ego and the necessity to not only have gratitude for what we already have, but wishing with the purest form of intention and the removal of ego. For you see, the more you allow your ego to become stronger, your life will progressively grow murkier.

Ladybugs & ladybirds

With the origin dating back to early settlers and farming communities, ladybugs were once viewed as blessings for a bountiful harvest for the farmers' crops. The ladybugs were responsible for eating the pests that would damage the crops and ensure a successful yield. This folklore transformed into a belief that if a ladybug lands on you, you need to close your eyes and make a wish and good luck will come to you.

Over time the legend expanded. Ladybugs are symbols of joyful spirits and abundance, and are believed to carry the power of creating new opportunities. Should you make a wish in their presence, they will open up their wings and fly away, generating bountiful magic in the air and the spawning of serendipitous pathways for you to encounter. All with the purpose of making your dreams come true. So the next time you encounter a ladybug, take a moment and remind yourself of the beauty of nature and the hidden powers within.

Loose eyelashes

I remain fascinated by this specific wishing ritual, as loose eyelashes seem particularly random. With rather ambiguous origins and various versions prevalent, one thing in common amongst them all is the fact that you cannot simply pull an eyelash out and make a wish. If you do, your wish will not come true (along with the known fact that we need eyelashes for eye protection, and the long length of time for them to grow back, I am not sure why anyone would even want to pull one out)!

Regardless, British and Irish folklore from the 18th century has it that if you lose an eyelash, you are to put it on the back of your hand, make a wish, and then wave your hand over your shoulder. If the eyelash leaves your hand, your wish is destined to come true.

Various other versions have you place the loose eyelash on other surfaces, such as the tip of your nose, where you simply blow it off in an upward fashion. If you are successful in moving it, your wish will be fulfilled.

Rub a laughing Buddha's belly

With his bald head, big round belly, open robe, and never ending smile, the Laughing Buddha is both easily recognizable and cherished worldwide. The beads around his neck symbolize wisdom and are better known as the 'Pearls of Wisdom'. Should your Laughing Buddha carry a cloth bag, the meaning varies, but traditionally it represents abundance for believers. Alternatively, Laughing Buddha uses the bag to collect all your worries and place them in his bag to lessen your load. Laughing Buddha with a wealth ball or golden nugget invites wealth. If he has a bowl above his head, he is inviting the heavens to bring abundance. His overall charismatic presence cannot help but make you feel good inside and ignite your inner spark.

There are many different versions, all with various virtues. Regardless of style, legend has it if you rub a Laughing Buddha's belly it will bring you good luck, happiness and prosperity.

Wishing stones

A very popular wishing ritual is that of wishing stones. Wishing stones come in all shapes and sizes, from mere pebbles, to tiny rocks of various shapes such as hearts, to moonstones, to crystals, and other lucky gemstones. Some are believed to carry special powers of healing, protection, and even play a role in feng shui. It is up to you to pick your own. All over the world people have also been known to write their wishes on stones. Sometimes the wishing stones are collected in dedicated wishing containers, sometimes a person will keep a wishing stone close by and hold it in a pocket, or sometimes the wish will be shared with another person and the wishing stone will be passed on as a gift for someone else to hold. Whatever you end up ultimately deciding to do with your wishing stone is up to you.

I encourage you to connect with nature and go on a wish adventure. Find a special stone on your way and write your wish on the stone. If you want to release your wishes back to the universe and you find yourself near a river, lake or ocean, hold your wishing stone in the palm of your hand, close your eyes, make your wish, and throw it into the water creating a ripple effect. The ripple effect will act as a multiplier to make your wishes proliferate and symbolically increase the odds of your wishing coming true.

So many more

There are so many more wish making rituals beyond what I have mentioned and they are echoed in stories and legends worldwide for thousands of years. Moreover, there are an overwhelming abundance of variations for each. Use these wishing ritual examples to create 'little wish reminders' for yourself to follow your passion and pursue your dreams.

There are so many mysteries that lie beyond. Our world is without end. So every time you go to bed at night, make a point of going outside or looking out your window, and look up the stars or the moon and take a few minutes to make a wish and visualize your dreams. Or when you are crossing a railroad track as a passenger in a vehicle, close your eyes, lift your feet and make a wish.

All these little daily reminders and wishing icons will ensure you never lose sight of your dreams and keep them forefront and centre. We are not all disciplined in our actions so it doesn't hurt to associate your wishes with rituals, symbols and actions that provide us with daily reminders to follow our passions. And if you are in the presence of others and they wonder what you are doing, simply tell them, *"I am making my wishes come true"*.

When will your wishes come true? You will never know until you try. My advice? Be creative. Make your own wishing rituals or start your own viral wishing trend! There are no rules as long as you maintain the basic principles of good and pure intention combined with gratitude. Wish more. Do more. And make our world a better place.

The universe has a
remarkable ability of
showing us signs.
Listen.

DAILY REMINDERS

Are you ready to embrace all that you have been given?

Wishing is truly a remarkable phenomenon spanning all cultures and generations throughout the history of humanity. After merely scratching the surface of some of the various types of wishing rituals that have been in existence for thousands of years, I hope you will begin to appreciate their inherent significance, value and ultimate contribution to all our technological advancements to date. You will understand that in fact, it is the fulfilled wishes of all humanity that have moved our societies forward one wish at a time – one wish built upon another.

And in the end, what can we observe from all these wishing rituals? That the world loves to wish. Since the earliest of civilizations, the human race simply loves to wish.

Wishing connects us all to each other, to our surrounding world and universe beyond. It is our natural instinct to wish and there is great universal power behind every wish. We were all born the ability to fulfill our innermost desires. As long as our hearts are in the right place, with good and pure intentions, wish making is a gift for us to practice and ultimately master. Wishing can enable you to believe in yourself and the power you have within. It takes dedication, concentration and the vision to see things through to completion.

Look at this as a moment in time to follow old wish traditions, or create new ones. It is an opportunity to reconnect with your childhood memories and cosmic intelligence. Time is precious - there is only so much time on the human quest for understanding and discovery. Don't waste it. All it takes to start is one wish.

All innovation derives from a wish

The beginning of a wish marks the beginning of a creation. All of creation and all innovation derived from a wish, a natural desire, a goal or task waiting to be fulfilled and realized. All ideas are formed within our brains, preconceived, prior to physical or actual completion. If you are able to envision it, you can create it. The ability to wish is the most remarkable gift we have but in order to experience the beauty of this gift, we need to both nurture it and use it.

The very act of stepping outside of your comfort zone is critical to your personal success and overall well-being. You have to be prepared for the entire journey from inception through to completion – even if it involves ups and downs. Know that the ups and downs are a natural part of life. They balance us out and provide us with wisdom and a healthier perspective on what matter most. As soon as you open up the door to a wish, you never know where it will lead you.

Wish revolution

With every exploratory step forward on the journey to fulfill our wishes, we open the door to limitless possibilities. The more we experience, the more we uncover, and the more we share with others. I believe we can, and we will, create a spiritual shift towards true fulfillment. We can all experience it in our lifetimes, but we need to accelerate the process now. We need to pay more attention to others, to signs, and to the world around us. We need to understand the benefits of the power of one, being at peace, having faith, and being in sync with the hidden flows of the world. Furthermore, we need to incorporate all of our learnings into our education system and our every day lives.

Let us all become both spiritual archaeologists and transcendent revolutionists. This is the start of something big. This is the start of a Wish Revolution. Let's all play our part and encourage others to do the same. And before we know it, the world will be a better place.

The shift

I believe we as a human race are undergoing a shift – a spiritual revolution and an opening of the consciousness intelligence. What we have all learned up until this point needs to be amended. Mother Nature is telling us we need to make a shift in our belief system in the way we think, work and act. All of our choices have a direct effect on our environment and we need to extend our abundant wishes to our surroundings. The more conscious we are of making good decisions, the better it will be for our world in its entirety.

Wish making spans all races and those of all ages throughout all humankind. It is a miraculous mystery that continues to live on in our souls despite the natural complexities of our environment. It is the fundamental underlying phenomenon that brings unity to all humanity and to all existence.

I hope this book inspires you to wish more, dream more and take action to make all of your wishes come true. I also hope it makes you think more, observe more, listen to that still small voice within your soul, and tune into what is really important.

Remember that against that lush velvet backdrop of our beautiful night's skies, highlighted by the bright sea of stars that sparkle like diamonds in the forefront, there are an infinite amount of wishes that are waiting to be fulfilled.

It all starts with one wish.

Every doodle
holds a wish.

WISH DOODLES

Before you embark on your wish journey, you need to take time to take inventory of everything that has prevented you from following your wishes up until now. You need to take stock of your fears, doubts, and all your hesitations and make time to heal and recharge your soul. You can't go back to yesterday, but you can acknowledge your past and change your future. You can also start this process at any given time.

To further prepare you for your wish journey, try our separate doodle book, *1 Wish: A Doodle Book* to help you use artistic expression to document your progress. Many research studies have proven that the human brain often prefers viewing images rather than text. Sometimes drawing an image to represent your feelings, rather than writing them down in a detailed formal sense, will help you capture your feelings as an iconic representation – and when you create these doodles, no one will truly understand their inner significance as much as you. Your doodles should be representative of your feelings and your thoughts, and serve as a quick reminder that the images used encompass a much larger and more complex personal meaning.

When we mindlessly find ourselves making little drawings or doodles, quite often they are very revealing of our innermost thoughts, desires, and wishes. Doodles are artistic expressions of where are minds are at, at any given point in time.

I believe every doodle holds a wish.

Positive mind.
Positive vibes.
Positive outcome.

WISH JOURNAL

Document your journey

We all make wishes but have you ever written them down? Quite often we make wishes for something that we genuinely desire, but we don't write them down. We presume we will remember them all, but the reality is that unless we record them in some manner we may forget. Think about how many wishes you have made in your lifetime. Have you ever written them down? Can you remember what you wished for over the years? Did any of them come true? And if so, when?

If your wishes are truly important, the first step on your journey to make them come true is to write them down. When you write your wishes down, you are more likely to fulfill them. The process of writing your wishes down will force you to articulate your thoughts and desires, and make them real. It will motivate you to focus, begin with one wish, take action, make a plan, and get it done.

To help you on your journey, try using our **1 Wish: 101 Wishes** journal. There's room for 101 entries with a 2-page spread. Using a separate journal or notebook is a great way to start the process of writing down your wishes, remember to keep your journal in a handy place to ensure you start recording your wishes as they come to you. Make it part of your regular routine. You will be surprised at how quickly your journal will fill up. And at the end of it all you will have your very own personalized 'Book of Wishes'. Keep it for yourself or share it with your family and friends. And when it fills up, start a new volume and in a few years time you will have your very own wish book anthology. Use it as a road map representing what you want to do with your life and the whiteprints you want to create.

A wish journal is just the beginning to start the process, initiate thoughts, and get you thinking. A wish journal is more of a high level bird's eye view – a home to document all your wishes in one place. To then take one of your wishes to the next level, you need to make it part of your everyday life and develop a bigger plan to make it happen. The larger the wish, the more detailed you need to be. Some wishes may even require a comprehensive project plan and an entire team behind you to make it happen. It's all up to you how big or small each of your wishes become.

Whatever you decide to wish for, and whatever wishing rituals you use to you make each wish, give yourself permission to achieve your goals. It's all about putting the energy out there, visualizing it, and using the powers of intention. When you make a wish don't overcomplicate it. Get back to the basics. Keep it simple. Stay on track and stay focused. Don't allow for distractions to get in your way. Continually re-evaluate your path to ensure your wishes are aligned with your choices in life.

Manifest your wishes

When you begin the process, say your wish and write it down as if it has already happened. Manifestation techniques may help your wishes to gain influence and strength. The more you truly believe in yourself and your wishes, the more likely you will actively work towards making them come true. Take notes along the way. Make sure you write fresh off every notable experience including challenges, lessons learned, opportunities created, milestones, results, those who help you, any moments you want to treasure and more, so that you remember all the important aspects and don't miss anything out. Write down all the helpful and useful information that will help you to move forward, open up the door to making new wishes, and share your wishes and experiences with others.

Your wish journal is truly about capturing all your innermost wishes, hopes and dreams down in one place. Once you begin, follow your heart, your natural instincts, and trust in yourself to believe. Fulfill all your passions with pure and wholesome intentions. Strengthen your ability to quickly recover when you encounter all the ups and downs, and success will follow. Use the power of choice to guide you along the way and know that even the tiniest of nudges can lead to you a vastly different destination – it's all up to you.

There is so much more than we will ever know in this life and there is no better time than now to explore. Our advancements in the more recent years have been exponential and I feel that within our lifetime here, right now, we have a high potential to release what has been hidden to us for years. Seek from within. Believe in you. Believe in others. Believe in the universe. And remember,

"Anything is possible if you put your mind to it".

Do what makes
your soul shine.

TATIANA COLHOUN

Eternal Optimist. Lover of Dreams. Entrepreneur.
Passionate about making a positive change in the world.

★

What do you wish for?